KAHLIL GIBRAN'S
THE PROPHET
AND
THE ART OF PEACE

KAHLIL GIBRAN'S
THE PROPHET
AND
THE ART OF PEACE

THE NEW ILLUSTRATED EDITION
OF KAHLIL GIBRAN'S TIMELESS WISDOM

WATKINS PUBLISHING
LONDON

Kahlil Gibran's *The Prophet and The Art of Peace*

This paperback edition first published in the United Kingdom and Ireland in 2011 by
Watkins Publishing, an imprint of Duncan Baird Publishers Ltd
Sixth Floor
Castle House
75–76 Wells Street
London W1T 3QH

Conceived, created and designed by Duncan Baird Publishers

Designer: Justin Ford
Picture Researcher: Julia Ruxton
Managing Editor: Christopher Westhorp
Managing Designer: Daniel Sturges

British Library Cataloguing-in-Publication Data:
A CIP record for this book is available from the British Library

ISBN: 978-1-78028-000-4

1 3 5 7 9 10 8 6 4 2

Typeset in Adobe Jenson Pro
Colour reproduction by Colourscan, Singapore
Printed in China by Imago

About the consultant
Joe Jenkins is the co-author, with Suheil Bushrui, of the acclaimed biography *Kahlil Gibran: Man and Poet* (1998). He is a former Research Fellow at the Kahlil Gibran Research and Studies Project at the University of Maryland.

Cover and page 2 captions
Cover art: An open hand, traditional symbol of knowledge, protection and peace.
Page 2: The central medallion of the Ardabil carpet, Iran, 16th century.
(Victoria and Albert Museum/V&A Images, London.)

Contents

INTRODUCTION:

The Timeless Wisdom of Kahlil Gibran 6

PART ONE:

The Prophet   24

PART TWO:

The Garden of the Prophet   150

PART THREE: FURTHER SELECTED WRITINGS 190

The Madman   192

The Forerunner   220

Sand and Foam   240

The Wanderer   258

CHRONOLOGY 266

FURTHER READING 267

INDEX 269

PICTURE CREDITS AND ACKNOWLEDGMENTS 271

Introduction
The Timeless Wisdom of Kahlil Gibran

Kahlil Gibran achieved lasting eminence and fame as a writer in two disparate cultures. A liberating force in Arabic literature, he also became one of the most widely read authors in English, his adopted tongue. His work possesses a distinctive flavour of ancient wisdom and mysticism, often leaving the reader surprised to discover that its creator lived in New York from 1912 to 1931. During a comparatively short life, from 1883 to 1931, millions of Arabic-speaking people came to consider him the genius of his age and in the West his work has been compared to Dante, Blake and Rodin.[1] His popularity as an Arab writer in the West was unprecedented and today *The Prophet* is one of the most highly regarded poems of modern times.

A Lebanese boyhood
Gibran Khalil Gibran, who became known as Kahlil Gibran, was born in the north of Lebanon on 6 January 1883. The village of his birth, Bisharri, is perched on a small plateau on cliffs beneath Mount Lebanon. Below the village are the famous ancient cedar groves of Wadi Qadisha, the sacred valley. Through history the cedars have been both a symbol and a source of life. The trees were used by the pharaohs to furnish their tombs and by King Solomon to construct his Great Temple in Jerusalem. The Phoenicians built great ocean-going vessels with the mighty trees and carried their weaves, purple dyes, glass and the phonetic alphabet to a barbarian world.

A 16th-century Ottoman hanging linen embroidered with silk thread.
The Ottomans were the imperial rulers of Gibran's Lebanese homeland.

Gibran's father Khalil, whose name the child inherited as his middle name (according to Arabic custom), was a tax-collector and his mother, Kamileh Rahmeh, was the daughter of a Maronite priest. Protected by the physical remoteness of the mountain region, the Christian Maronites had preserved a liturgy conducted in the Aramaic tongue of Jesus. The legends surrounding Saint Marun and the many mystics who had lived in the mountains were palpable to the young Gibran as he played in the secret caves, mysterious grottoes, monasteries and temples hewn out of the side of Mount Lebanon.

Under the shadow of the great mountain, Kamileh and her husband reared their family. Although life was hard it was not unendurable and the rugged and resourceful villagers eked out a living on the thin crust of soil left by the heavy winter snows. However, only a generation before, another more terrifying shadow had been cast upon the minds and in the memories of the people of Lebanon when the country had been propelled into a terrible civil war.[2]

With the Ottoman Empire appearing to weaken, a fear of foreign intervention began to mount. Sectarian violence broke out and in 1860 thousands of Christians were massacred in just four weeks. Up to then many faith groups – Chaldean, Greek and Syriac Catholics; Greek and Syriac Orthodox; Armenian, Assyrian, Jacobite, Maronite and Nestorian Christians; Shi'ite, Sunni and Druze Muslims; and Jews – had lived together in a region which, perhaps more than any other, had been a meeting point of East and West. The turmoil generated by this explosion of violence etched a deep scar on the consciousness of the people of Lebanon. During this period of reciprocal destruction the villagers of Bisharri reverted back to their ancient instinct for survival and retreated to the impregnable fortress of the mountain. Although his immediate kin had escaped the bloodshed, haunting memories remained with Gibran all his life.[3]

He never forgot, either, the dramatic beauty of the places he had known as a child, which after his exile in 1894 became the object of his yearning and a constant source of his inspiration. The seeds of this exile had been sown over a number of years by a father who had frittered away his income and by a mother intent on improving her children's future. Driven by the classic urges of escaping poverty and tribal or religious repression, many Lebanese families before Kamileh had taken their families away and sailed for America – their resolve strengthened by an ancient tradition known as *al-mahjar* of travelling to the city (a place of prosperity and hope) in search of a better way of life.

Growing up in exile

Despite the hardship of the seething tenements in Boston's Chinatown during the 1890s, Kamileh was intent on nurturing her son's artistic talent, which had become manifest to those outside the close-knit family when, as a fifteen-year-old, he was chosen to illustrate the cover of an edition of *Omar Khayyám, The Tentmaker*. The young artist found himself in Boston at a propitious time. The city's charitable organizations had realized that something had to be done for the poor and had recently set about establishing settlement houses run by social workers. It was at one of these in 1896 that Gibran's drawings caught the eye of an art teacher.

Word spread and soon the youngster found himself propelled into bohemian Boston. With his modest manners, good looks, and unique talent, this particular "street fakir"[4] endeared himself to the city's intellectual and artistic circles. Metaphorically, he had crossed the railroad tracks into "Brahmin Boston", where a new showpiece of culture, the Boston Public Library, had recently opened in an atmosphere still throbbing from the transcendentalist chords struck by its own son Ralph Waldo Emerson. At this time avant-garde enclaves rebelled against the sentimentality of the "sick little end of the century"[5] and dabbled with exotica, spiritualism and orientalism against a backdrop of Turkish carpets, jade bowls, waterpipes, fezzes, pointed slippers and Maeterlinck's neoplatonic broodings on death and pre-ordained love.[6]

In 1904 Gibran had his first exhibition. One of the many admirers who came to see what the *Boston Evening Transcript* called "the ponderous beauty and nobility of his art"[7] was Mary Haskell, a progressive headmistress from South Carolina. On first meeting Gibran she found him, "electrifying . . . mobile like a flame . . . *the Pulse* visible".[8]

During those early years in Boston, as Gibran watched his sister and brother die of tuberculosis and his mother of cancer, it was his "guardian angel"[9] Mary Haskell who consoled him and reassured him that he was "not a stranger in a strange land".[10] He was later to write to Mary: "Three things in my life have done most for me: My mother who let me alone; you, who had faith in me and in my work; and my father, who called out the fighter in me".[11]

The creation of the writer

Mary's role is so crucial to Gibran's development as a writer that at times biographers find two destinies weaved as one. Although it would be many years before her protégé's poetry and art was acknowledged, her faith in and generosity towards "the Syrian genius" never wavered.[12] Their relationship was an intellectual and deeply emotional "kinship", and, although not without its difficulties, Mary remained a loyal friend right through his life.

In 1908, and with Mary's patronage, Gibran enrolled at the École des Beaux-Arts and the Académie Julian in Paris, which Gibran called "The City of Light".[13] After his studies, he would sit and drink in the *zeitgeist* of the Latin Quarter, participating in late-night discussions on Fauvism, Rodin, revolution, Tolstoy, Cubism and Nietzsche whose *Thus Spake Zarathustra* was revolutionizing the literary sensibilities of the age. The last has most importance for Gibran, as he had audaciously adopted the towering figure of a prophet from the East as his mouthpiece.[14]

Boston felt provincial after his return from Paris and Mary arranged for him to move to New York where he settled in his "hermitage" on 51 West Tenth Street in Greenwich Village. For the rest of his life it was here that he would work, often until dawn, to bring his twin crafts to perfection in a punishing routine fortified by strong coffee and cigarettes, and in later life alcohol. He wrote to Mary: "It seems that I was born with an arrow in my heart and it is painful to *pull it* and painful to *leave it*".[15]

The outbreak of war in Europe in 1914 fired concern for his homeland and he helped organize a relief committee to combat the famine that ravaged Lebanon, and in an "Open Letter to Islam" he called on the various sects in Ottoman-occupied lands to cease their internecine struggles. Gibran's writings at this time began to be published extensively in the Arab world and an anthology of his works, from 1912 to 1918, was collected under the title *Al-'Awasif* (*The Tempests*). In it there is a whip in his words as the poet condemns religious fundamentalism, misogyny, oppression and inequality, his heroes the *fellahin*, the downtrodden and oppressed, who against all odds proclaim a message of peace and justice. The combination of a Rousseau-like belief in the innate goodness of an unshackled humanity and a hitherto unique interpretation of the Christian message had led him to launch a radical assault on Church and State in *'Ara'is al-Muruj* (*Nymphs of the Valley*, 1906) and *Al-Arwah al-Mutamarridah* (*Spirits Rebellious*, 1908). Such attacks represented the wildest insubordination and Gibran was vilified and condemned as a heretic – there was a public burning of his books in Beirut and he was excommunicated from the Maronite church.[16] Nevertheless, his huge popularity among ordinary readers and literary critics led to him being acknowledged as the foremost writer in contemporary Arab literature – his works having instigated a renaissance in Arabic creativity in a "rebellion" akin to that in England a century earlier when Blake, Wordsworth and Shelley strove to explore the literature of internalized quest and Promethean aspiration.[17]

The expression of alienation so eloquently espoused in Gibran's works became not merely geographically orientated but an expression of a soul descended into the corrupting realm of matter, and his vitriol was directed not just at the unbecoming influences in his homeland but also at the universally defiled image of a spiritual emigrant in the "heart of darkness".[18]

The universality of these convictions was to resonate with the public and at the end of the war *The Madman* was published. In the thirty-five prose poems and parables, Gibran continued his theme of a world defiled by the "new primitives" intent on making liberty "a cadaverous spectre".[19] Like the characters in the literature of Shakespeare, Blake and the Sufis, Gibran uses the figure of a "madman" as his mouthpiece – an inspired poet-seer – who through irony and paradox leads the reader from the visible to the invisible, from untruth to truth.

The discernible tendency of *The Madman* is the purging of the conditioned values which prevent man from realizing his Greater Self, for according to Sufi teachings man has no fixed nature, no unity, only masks. In "The Seven Selves" (see page 196) different personalities rebel against the "madman" who, despite the chaos, remains watching; for it is this madman who knows of the existence of the "Greater Self" – "The Greater Sea" (see page 206) which is distinguished from the "great sea" – "pessimists" "optimists," "philanthropists," "mystics", "idealists," "realists," and the "religious fundamentalists" the "most deadly" of all. The madman wants to "bathe", free of judgment, or "naked", in this Great Sea away from the shore where those absorbed in minutiae pick up dead fish, throw salt into the sea, trace shadows on the sand, scoop up the foam, their heads "buried in the sand".[20] In "The Astronomer" (see page 260) another madman makes the transition from multiplicity and towards unity as an inner journey is explored: "Then he placed his hand upon his breast saying, 'I watch all these suns and moons and stars.'"[21]

Given what the world had just endured during its four-year orgy of reciprocal destruction, *The Madman* was an opportune work with which to introduce himself to the Western world and its impact was immediate with the book being translated into French, Italian and Russian within a year of publication.

Journals of this time reveal a diminutive man, sometimes dressed in Dervish robes, splattered with paint, and at others in his Irish homespun suit or attired like a cultured Frenchman. He was a consummate creator who believed "there is nothing more tiresome than laziness" and only found freedom in his work (his "love made visible"), thus in 1920 Gibran produced another collection of parables, *The Forerunner: His Parables and Poems*, again using madmen like "The King-Hermit" (see page 226) as his mouthpieces.[22]

In *The Forerunner* Gibran explores the Sufi idea of *shawq*, man's ontological yearning for and journeying towards the divine.[23] A "madman", the king-hermit can no longer be ruler over those who assumed his vices and attribute to him their virtues and so he leaves the clamour and duality of the city for the forest and unity. The theme of journeying towards union is continued in "Out of my Deeper Heart" (see page 230) in which a bird flies from the forerunner's heart: "Higher and higher did it rise, yet larger and larger did it grow. . . . Yet it left not my heart".[24] The final parable, "The Last Watch" (see page 234), deals with the reception afforded *The Forerunner*. Gibran told Mary Haskell that in this piece was "a promise", and whereas *The Madman* ends with the bitterest thing in it, *The Forerunner* ends with the sweetest: "He who calls himself echo to a voice yet unheard".[25]

With the Last Watch closing and the darkness of war retreating, Gibran observed a new world being born around him. When the war had ended he had written to Mary: "Out of the dark mist a new world is born . . . The air is crowded with the sound of rushing waters and the beating of Mighty Wings. The voice of God is in the wind."[26] At the age of thirty-seven, fired by his passionate belief in the unity of being, Gibran was, at last, ready to bring to fruition his earlier promise: "I came to say a word and I shall utter it . . . That which alone I do today shall be proclaimed before the people in days to come."[27] The forerunner was waiting, as was his creator, for, "he who calls himself echo to a voice yet unheard".

The Prophet is born

Three years earlier, Gibran had written to Mary about that "echo": "This prophet had already 'written' me before I attempted to 'write' him, had created me before I created him. I have sought *The Prophet* ever since I was sixteen years old and now I am becoming conscious of his truths. He is the ripening of all my life."[28] There is little doubt that *The Prophet* – Gibran's masterpiece – is intensely personal, thinly veiled by names: Gibran, Almustafa; New York, Orphalese; Mary Haskell, Almitra; Lebanon, Almustafa's isle of birth; and the twelve years in Orphalese the twelve years spent in New York prior to the publication of the book.

Almustafa preaches twenty-six poetic sermons on a wide range of human subjects, ranging from love, joy and sorrow, freedom, good and evil, to prayer, religion and death. The occasion for these is his final departure from the land of Orphalese, which he leaves with sadness, for he has given the people much of himself. It is Almitra, the seeress, who begs him to "give us of your truth". She is aware, too, of his "longing for the land of your memories." Almustafa's departure for "the isle of his birth" symbolizes his return to the unborn state from which, as he promises at the end, he will again be reincarnated. "A little while, a moment of rest upon the wind, and another woman shall bear me."

Gibran awaited his moment for publication and wrote to Mary: "Human beings have changed remarkably during the past three years. They are hungry for beauty, for truth."[29] He was proved right when within a month of publication in 1923 all 1,300 copies of the first edition were sold, setting in motion a trend that continues to this day. In an age when it was impossible to generate by intensive publicity the kind of sales which modern bestsellers enjoy, it was quickly apparent that the public were genuinely moved by Gibran's impulse to sing from the heart. Not since *The Arabian Nights* had a writer of Arab descent enjoyed such universal appeal and *The Prophet*, the "strange little book" as he called it, went on to outsell all others in the twentieth century except the Bible.[30]

It had taken Gibran many years to assiduously perfect the unity of a message which he mirrored through text and pictures, an expression of the "sacredness" of his "inner life", and it came as no surprise to those around him when he was mentioned in the same breath as William Blake. At the heart of this "strange little book" is the message that while love can be wounding and painful, it can also lift to ecstasy. Truth, liberation and union with the Supreme Identity which *is* Love, is possible through aspiration and yearning. Life is a journey and Love is both departure and destination. "Like a procession you walk together towards your god-self", says Almustafa in one sermon (see page 74) – the insistence being on the essential identity of love and pain, which evidently contained real personal significance for Gibran.

The grief and alienation experienced by the hypersensitive youth had laid its stamp on him, attuning his subconscious to the "most delicate light and shade" and prompting him to sing with the eloquence of Isaiah and the sorrow of Jeremiah.[31] One critic described Gibran's work as being "dipped in blood . . . a cry bursting through a wounded heart", and asked of those who wish to understand him to "imagine for themselves what a degree of pain it would require to inspire them as did that suffering which so inspired Gibran".[32]

Almustafa speaks first on love (see page 37), and this is perhaps the most outstandingly beautiful of all his sermons: "Love has no other desire but to fulfil itself. But if you love and must needs have desires, let these be your desires: To melt and be like a running brook that sings its melody to the night. To know the pain of too much tenderness. To be wounded by your own understanding of love; And to bleed willingly and joyfully."[33]

Barely 20,000 words long, philosophical in nature and mystical in tone, *The Prophet* was hardly a book one would expect to capture the attention of the reading public. Yet eventually it did. Its author began to be "overwhelmed" with admiring letters about the book. *The New York Times* on publication was reminded of "Gautama, the philosophers of the *Upanishads* . . .

and the best of the old Hebrew prophets", other reviews wrote of its ". . . extraordinary dramatic power, deep erudition, lightning-like intuition, lyrical lift and metrical mastery with which the message is presented, and the beauty, beauty, beauty, which permeates the entire pattern".[34] The Irish poet George Russell (who wrote under the pseudonym Æ) observed: "I could quote from every page, and from every page I could find some beautiful and liberating thought".[35] On publication, Gibran himself told Mary: "The whole Prophet is saying just one thing: 'You are far far greater than you know and all is well.'"[36]

For many *The Prophet* represented the height of Gibran's literary career and given its importance in his oeuvre it is not surprising that some critics thought his works leading up to it were exploratory, even rudimentary.[37] But another view takes his Arabic works, such as *Iram, The City of Lofty Pillars,* published in 1921 two years before *The Prophet,* and his English works, such as *The Madman,* on their own terms by giving due regard in *Iram* to the exploration of the Sufi principle of the Unity of Being (*wahdat al-wudjud*) and in *The Madman* to the elevation of the outsider-poet-seer. In his earlier works, too, there are hints and intimations of his literary aim of merging Muslim and Christian mystical heritages, a dream now realized in his portrayal of Almustafa, the eponymous prophet, both a Christ-like figure and the universal man of Muslim civilization.

There is no doubt that *The Prophet* occupies a unique place in world literature, which makes an assessment of its true value a difficult task for the critic. Often unjustly branded as a romanticized version of universal philosophical and religious teachings, it has in some ways been a victim of its own astonishing success. The reality is that it is a work of remarkable compassion, insight and hope, with a timeless message, phrased with a simplicity and rhythmical quality that renders it accessible to a wide readership. Effortless, but deeply felt, Gibran's perspicuous prose is the fruit of a lifetime's dedication to perfecting an instrument whereby he could communicate to others, in the most effective and beautiful manner possible, the unseen order which he believed to be at the heart of everything on earth.

With its sensational success Gibran found himself propelled onto a world stage where he would appropriate a variety of personas that enchanted and sometimes beguiled his acquaintances and audiences. Given his chameleon-like ease of adaptiveness, one journalist wrote, "Gibran is Broadway or Copley Square or The Strand or the Avenue de L'Opera, a correctly dressed cosmopolitan of the Western world . . . a sensible denizen of Greenwich Village for such there be",[38] while another onlooker thought that the short man with his white suit, hat and cane was "the spitting image" of another immigrant of the time, Charlie Chaplin.[39] Beneath the masks, however, was a man whose gestures were those of "the unhurried courtesy of the East", an artist capable of transcending the barriers between East and West who could justifiably call himself, although a Lebanese and a patriot, a citizen of the world. It was as a man from Lebanon that he spoke and it was a Lebanese mode of thought and belief he ardently expressed. His words went beyond the mere evocation of the mysterious East but endeavoured to communicate the necessity of reconciling Christianity and Islam.

Fame, poor health and twilight years

After completing *The Prophet*, Gibran had just seven years to live, yet the exhilaration of unburdening himself threw his mysterious illness into the shadows for a short while and he wrote to a friend that his ailment had "forsaken" him and he was in good spirits despite the grey streaks traced on his hair.[40]

As his fame grew so did his social circle and he met, sometimes painted, the actress Sarah Bernhardt, the spiritual leader of the Bahá'í faith 'Abdu'l-Bahá, the psychologist Carl Gustav Jung, the poet W.B. Yeats, the Mexican painter José Clemente Orozco, the composer Claude Debussy and the writers John Galsworthy and G.K. Chesterton. But despite the acclaim generated by the spectacular success of *The Prophet*, Gibran's latter years were difficult. As more self-appointed devotees of "Gibranism" learned that the "Lebanese savant" was living on West Tenth Street, he began to be inundated with visitors.[41] While some came to confess, or be comforted, and some came seeking counsel, others came simply out of curiosity. Gibran himself had no desire to wear the mantle of a prophet: "The difference between a prophet and a poet," he wrote, "is that the prophet lives what he teaches – and the poet does not."[42]

In his next published work Gibran expressed his ambivalent feelings towards fame: "Fame is the shadow of passion standing in the light".[43] (See page 254.) Although he described it as a "stop-gap" work, the 300 aphorisms in *Sand and Foam* include some memorable sayings. While many echo Almustafa's words and could almost be footnotes to his sermons, the predominant influence is that of William Blake, a master of aphorism.[44]

In 1928 Gibran published his longest work *Jesus, the Son of Man* – seventy-eight different impressions of Jesus presented imaginatively in the form of accounts attributed to his contemporaries, placing entirely fictitious characters alongside the disciples, the Virgin Mary and Mary Magdalene and presenting the views of "anti-heroes" such as Caiaphas, Pontius Pilate and Barabbas, who makes the rueful remark that: "His crucifixion endured but for an hour. But I shall be crucified unto the end of my years."[45] In the months running up to its publication Gibran had been suffering from what he called "summer rheumatism", ominously revealing that the medics, in their desperation, were trying "electric" treatment for his "mysterious ailment".[46] But, although it was to be his last successful work, *Jesus, the Son of Man* is not the anguished cry of a failing man but a breathtaking testament of a poet whose soaring prose continued to rail against the dying of the light.

Constantly wracked with pain Gibran resorted to alcohol to numb it, and as the cruel winter winds blasted their way onto the eastern seaboard, the poet struggled, alone in his "Hermitage" in New York, to come to terms with the reality of a terminal condition. To the outside world he put on a brave face and announced that his next book, *The Garden of The Prophet*, was to be published that autumn. However, he did not live to see its publication and turned instead to a work the seeds of which had been sown twenty years previously. The epic scale of this work, *The Earth Gods*, is reminiscent of Keats' last poem "Hyperion".[47] It is a discussion held by three gods: one is pessimistic about the meaning of the unending cycle of life and death; the second encourages a spiritual quest to find the meaning; but the third, the youngest of the trio, moderates the debate by counselling acceptance of their predicament and expounding that "only love gives meaning". Although the book highlighted the all-embracing power of love, the prevailing mood is sombre and reflects the mellow resignation of a dying man, sometimes causing the work to come across as a didactic piece dressed in literary finery.[48]

When the Great Depression of the 1930s began, Gibran's growing fame and fortune must have appeared enviable to many. As his books were going through new editions and his English works were being translated, his royalties continued to increase.[49] A lecture bureau offered to take him on a reading tour and rarely a day went by when the mail, telegraph or telephone didn't bring fresh testimonies of appreciation. Publishers, no doubt wary of possible cataclysmic days ahead, pressed their authors for new work and Gibran began to put the finishing touches to *The Wanderer*, a work he had begun in Boston three years previously.[50]

Gibran's "wanderer" is a poet-seer introduced as a youth with a veil of pain upon his pale face, now incarcerated in a madhouse by "those who live in the madhouse on the other side of the wall".[51] Again, as in previous short works, despite the critical analysis of the so-called civilized world a message of unity and hope pervades, particularly in the last poem "The River" (see page 264) – a source of luminosity and rapture, the confluence of river with sea a metaphor for the union of individuality into the Absolute, the Greater Self returning to its source.[52]

The poem symbolizes the course of human life and is eloquent testimony to Gibran's power as a writer, summing up his view of life in an open, straightforward manner, and the imagery is so simple that it could have come straight from a children's story.

Gibran died in 1931 and was laid to rest in the grotto of the little monastery of Mar-Sarkis near Bisharri. Nine months later *The Garden of The Prophet* was published – Almustafa returns after twelve years to the isle of his birth. In the hush of the garden where his mother and father are buried he speaks: "Now, today, to be is to be wise, though not a stranger to the foolish; it is to be strong, but not to the undoing of the weak; to play with young children, not as fathers, but rather as playmates who would learn their games".[53] "The image of the morning sun in a dewdrop is not less than the sun. . . . You and the stone are one. There is a difference only in heart-beats. Your heart beats a little faster, does it, my friend? Ay, but it is not so tranquil."[54]

In an epoch characterized as the Age of Anxiety, Gibran saw a divine order infused in the world. And his consistency in proclaiming these views when similar schools of thought were retreating in disorder before the massed battalions of materialism, mechanization and militarism surely foreshadowed the resilience and fortitude displayed by his countrymen after his death – a people who, in the face of devastating and convulsive upheavals, have stood firm in defence of the values enunciated by Gibran, and, with unflinching resolve, continue to proclaim his message, the message of Lebanon, to an unheeding world.

Gibran is the most successful and famous Arab writer in the world. Despite the comfort offered by technological achievements and the insights afforded by analysis (and the benefits of either are much disputed), the modern psyche still has a wound in its soul. Gibran's message is a healing one and his quest to understand the tensions between spirit and exile anticipated the needs of an age witnessing the spiritual and intellectual impasse of modernity itself. His writings reveal the penetrating vision of a seer, who, without crusading or preaching, warned of the terrible dangers that befall an epoch intent on border-consciousness, material greed and blistering yet blind change. The wisdom set forth in the form of a simple, lyrical beauty and a profound depth of meaning, for all who endeavour to seek it, applies with striking timelessness to the momentous challenges we face today.

JOE JENKINS

NOTES TO THE INTRODUCTION

[1] Martin L. Wolf in the Preface to *Secrets of The Heart* by Kahlil Gibran, translated by Anthony Rizcallah Ferris, p.v; *Gibran Love Letters*, p.16.

[2] Kahlil S. Hawi, *Khalil Gibran: His Background, Character and Works*, p.25. N. Naimy, "The Mind and Thought of Kahlil Gibran" in *Journal of Arabic Literature*, 5, 1974. p.20 and p.21.

[3] From "A Speech by Khalil the Heretic", translated by Suheil Bushrui, in *An Introduction to Kahlil Gibran*, p.23 and p.26.

[4] Jessie Fremont Beale to Fred Holland Day, 25 November 1908.

[5] The phrase was used by Louise Guiney in a letter to Louise Chandler Moulton, 10 September 1894. It is explored in Stephen Maxfield Parrish's "Currents of the Nineties in Boston and London: Fred Holland Day, Louise Imogen Guiney and Their Circle". Unpublished Ph.D. dissertation, Harvard University, 1954.

[6] Count Maeterlinck (1862–1949) was a Belgian poet, playwright, and essayist awarded the Nobel Prize in Literature in 1911.

[7] *Boston Evening Transcript*, 3 May 1904, p.10.

[8] Otto, *Letters*, p.225.

[9] Mikhail Naimy, *Kahlil Gibran*, p. 60.

[10] Otto, *Letters*, p.3.

[11] Hilu, V. *Beloved Prophet: The Love Letters of Kahlil Gibran and Mary Haskell and her Private Journal*, p.418.

[12] Lebanon, at this time, was considered to be part of Greater Syria.

[13] Kahlil Gibran to Ameen Guraieb, 12 February 1908, in *A Self-Portrait*, p.9.

[14] Mikhail Naimy, *Kahlil Gibran*, p.89. Rodin introduced Gibran to the "twin muses" of William Blake, whose benign influence was to fall on Gibran's writings and art. In respect of Nietzsche, see Otto *Letters*, p.68.

[15] Otto, *Letters*, p.147.

[16] Kahlil Gibran, *Kahlil Gibran, A Self-Portrait*, pp.15–16 and Kahlil Gibran in *Spirits Rebellious*, pp.103–104.

[17] As founder-president of The Pen Bond (*al-Rabita al-Qalamiyyah*), "a small and rather select group of avant-garde men of letters", Gibran and his associates began to liberate Arabic poetry from stupour – See S.K. Jayyusi, *Trends and*

Movements in Modern Arabic Poetry, 2 vols., p.91, p.94, p.96 and p.102. *Romantic Poetry and Prose*, edited by Harold Bloom and Lionel Tring, p.9.

[18] Kahlil Gibran in *A Tear and A Smile*, p.75.

[19] Kahlil Gibran in "The Tempest" in *A Treasury of Kahlil Gibran*, p.20, and "The Giants" in *Thoughts and Meditations*, p.84.

[20] The "sea" symbolizes the Great Spirit or Greater Self. Gibran wrote to Mary Haskell in February 1912, of "the Great Sea which we call God" (B.P., p. 61.) *The Madman*, pp.21–23.

[21] *The Madman*, p.61.

[22] Kahlil Gibran to Mariita Lawson, letter, 26 September 1921.

[23] The idea of "longing" is also to be found in Christian mysticism, for example in a classic text *The Cloud of Unknowing*, London, Penguin, 1961, p.68.

[24] Birds in various spiritual traditions are mediators between heaven and earth and embodiments of the soul. Kahlil Gibran, *The Forerunner: His Parables and Poems*, p.31.

[25] See Anne Salem Otto, *The Parables of Kahlil Gibran: An Interpretation of His Writings and His Art*, p.81. Also, Hilu, V. *Beloved Prophet*, p.53, p.61 and p.391.

[26] Hilu, V. *Beloved Prophet*, p.318.

[27] Kahlil Gibran, *A Tear and A Smile*, p.197.

[28] Suheil B. Bushrui and S.H. al-Kuzbari (eds and trans.), *Gibran Love Letters*, p.23 (9 November 1919) and Hilu, V. *Beloved Prophet*, p.328.

[29] Hilu, V. *Beloved Prophet*, p.300.

[30] "Strange little book" is cited by Mikhail Naimy quoting Gibran in *Aramco World*, XV, 6, p.11.

[31] George Kheirallah "The Life of Gibran Khalil Gibran" in *The Procession*, p.17.

[32] Introduction to *The Prophet* by Sarwat Okasha (into Arabic), Cairo, Dar al-Maaref, 1959.

[33] Suheil Bushrui and Joe Jenkins, *Kahlil Gibran: Man and Poet*, pp.75–76.

[34] Stanton A. Goblentz, "Gibran's Companion to The Prophet", from *The New York Times Book Review*, 10 June 1934, and Claude Bragdon in "Gibran: a Modern Prophet from Lebanon", in *Merely Players*, quoted in *Kahlil Gibran: Essays and Introductions*, p.25.

[35] George Russell (AE), *The Living Torch*, p.169.

[36] Chapel Hill Papers, 30 May 1922.

[37] See Mikhail Naimy "Gibran at his peak" in *Gibran of Lebanon: New Papers*, edited by Suheil Bushrui and Paul Gotch, p.3 and p.4.

[38] Joseph Gollomb, "An Arabian Poet in New York", *N.Y. Evening Post*, 29 March 1919, book section, p.1 and p.10.

[39] Marzieh Gail, *Other People, Other Places*, p.229.

[40] *Gibran Love Letters* (2 December 1923), p.71.

[41] See Martin L. Wolf in Editor's Preface to *A Treasury of Kahlil Gibran*, translated from the Arabic by Anthony Rizcallah Ferris, p.xi.

[42] Hilu, V. *Beloved Prophet*, p.397.

[43] Kahlil Gibran, *Sand and Foam*, p.41.

[44] Mikhail Naimy, *Kahlil Gibran: A Biography*, p.207. Some of the aphorisms were translated from Arabic and had already received publication in that language, for example in *al-Bayati wa'l-Tarayif* ("Beautiful and Rare Sayings"), published in 1923.

[45] Kahlil Gibran, *Jesus, the Son of Man*, p.190.

[46] Kahlil Gibran to Mariita Lawson, 8 September 1926.

[47] Hawi (p.175) found references to Keats in Gibran's notebooks of 1904. Gibran wrote a poem about Keats entitled *"Bihurouf min Nar"* ("With Letters of Fire"), which was published in *A Tear and A Smile* (1914). See also John Keats in *Hyperion: Book 1, The Oxford Anthology of English Literature: Romantic Poetry and Prose*, Oxford University Press, 1973, p.505.

[48] Kahlil Gibran, *The Earth Gods*, p.25 and p.37; the third god, like the youth in *Al-Mawakib* (*The Procession*), views love not pantheistically but particularly in the love between man and woman. (Hawi, p.238.) See also Bushrui and Jenkins, *Kahlil Gibran: Man and Poet*, p.273 and p.274.

[49] To date the poetry of Gibran has been translated into more than twenty languages.

[50] Otto, *Letters*, p.673.

[51] Kahlil Gibran, *The Wanderer: His Parables and his Sayings*, p.38.

[52] Gibran, like his contemporary T.S. Eliot, felt the "river within". T.S. Eliot writes: "The river is within us, the sea is all about us", in *Four Quartets*, (The Dry Salvages 1:15), London, Faber and Faber, 1943, p.25. See also Kahlil Gibran, *The Wanderer*, pp.82–83.

[53] Kahlil Gibran, *The Garden of The Prophet*, p.34.

[54] Ibid., p.23 and p.26.

PART ONE

The Prophet

Contents

The Coming of the Ship 26

Love 34

Marriage 38

Children 42

Giving 46

Eating and Drinking 50

Work 54

Joy and Sorrow 58

Houses 62

Clothes 66

Buying and Selling 68

Crime and Punishment 72

Laws 78

Freedom 82

Reason and Passion 86

Pain 90

Self-Knowledge 94

Teaching 98

Friendship 100

Talking 104

Time 108

Good and Evil 112

Prayer 116

Pleasure 120

Beauty 124

Religion 128

Death 132

The Farewell 136

CHAPTER ONE

The Coming of the Ship

Almustafa, the chosen and the beloved, who was a dawn unto his own day, had waited twelve years in the city of Orphalese for his ship that was to return and bear him back to the isle of his birth.

And in the twelfth year, on the seventh day of Ielool, the month of reaping, he climbed the hill without the city walls and looked seaward; and he beheld his ship coming with the mist.

Then the gates of his heart were flung open, and his joy flew far over the sea. And he closed his eyes and prayed in the silences of his soul.

But as he descended the hill, a sadness came upon him, and he thought in his heart:

How shall I go in peace and without sorrow? Nay, not without a wound in the spirit shall I leave this city.

Long were the days of pain I have spent within its walls, and long were the nights of aloneness; and who can depart from his pain and his aloneness without regret?

Too many fragments of the spirit have I scattered in these streets, and too many are the children of my longing that walk naked among these hills, and I cannot withdraw from them without a burden and an ache.

A 16th-century ceramic plate from Iznik adorned with the characteristic galleys of the Ottoman fleet.

It is not a garment I cast off this day, but a skin that I tear with my own hands.

Nor is it a thought I leave behind me, but a heart made sweet with hunger and with thirst.

Yet I cannot tarry longer.

The sea that calls all things unto her calls me, and I must embark.

For to stay, though the hours burn in the night, is to freeze and crystallize and be bound in a mould.

Fain would I take with me all that is here. But how shall I?

A voice cannot carry the tongue and the lips that gave it wings. Alone must it seek the ether.

And alone and without his nest shall the eagle fly across the sun.

Now when he reached the foot of the hill, he turned again towards the sea, and he saw his ship approaching the harbour, and upon her prow the mariners, the men of his own land.

And his soul cried out to them, and he said:

Sons of my ancient mother, you riders of the tides,

How often have you sailed in my dreams. And now you come in my awakening, which is my deeper dream.

Ready am I to go, and my eagerness with sails full set awaits the wind.

Only another breath will I breathe in this still air, only another loving look cast backward,

Then I shall stand among you, a seafarer among seafarers.

And you, vast sea, sleepless mother,

Who alone are peace and freedom to the river and the stream,

Only another winding will this stream make, only another murmur in this glade,

And then I shall come to you, a boundless drop to a boundless ocean.

And as he walked he saw from afar men and women leaving their fields and their vineyards and hastening towards the city gates.

And he heard their voices calling his name, and shouting from field to field telling one another of the coming of his ship.

And he said to himself:

Shall the day of parting be the day of gathering?

And shall it be said that my eve was in truth my dawn?

And what shall I give unto him who has left his plough in midfurrow, or to him who has stopped the wheel of his winepress?

Shall my heart become a tree heavy-laden with fruit that I may gather and give unto them?

And shall my desires flow like a fountain that I may fill their cups?

Am I a harp that the hand of the mighty may touch me, or a flute that his breath may pass through me?

A seeker of silences am I, and what treasure have I found in silences that I may dispense with confidence?

If this is my day of harvest, in what fields have I sowed the seed, and in what unremembered seasons?

If this indeed be the hour in which I lift up my lantern, it is not my flame that shall burn therein.

Empty and dark shall I raise my lantern,

And the guardian of the night shall fill it with oil and he shall light it also.

These things he said in words. But much in his heart remained unsaid. For he himself could not speak his deeper secret.

And when he entered into the city all the people came to meet him, and they were crying out to him as with one voice. And the elders of the city stood forth and said:
Go not yet away from us.
A noontide have you been in our twilight, and your youth has given us dreams to dream.
No stranger are you among us, nor a guest, but our son and our dearly beloved.
Suffer not yet our eyes to hunger for your face.

And the priests and the priestesses said unto him:
Let not the waves of the sea separate us now, and the years you have spent in our midst become a memory.
You have walked among us a spirit, and your shadow has been a light upon our faces.
Much have we loved you. But speechless was our love, and with veils has it been veiled.
Yet now it cries aloud unto you, and would stand revealed before you.
And ever has it been that love knows not its own depth until the hour of separation.

And others came also and entreated him. But he answered them not. He only bent his head; and those who stood near saw his tears falling upon his breast.

And he and the people proceeded towards the great square before the temple. And there came out of the sanctuary a woman whose name was Almitra. And she was a seeress.

And he looked upon her with exceeding tenderness, for it was she who had first sought and believed in him when he had been but a day in their city.

Noah's Ark, from The Fine Flower of Histories, *or* Zubdat al-Tawarikh, *a world history by Seyyid Loqman Ashuri, 1583.*

And she hailed him, saying:

Prophet of God, in quest of the uttermost, long have you searched the distances for your ship.

And now your ship has come, and you must needs go.

Deep is your longing for the land of your memories and the dwelling-place of your greater desires; and our love would not bind you nor our needs hold you.

Yet this we ask ere you leave us, that you speak to us and give us of your truth.

And we will give it unto our children, and they unto their children, and it shall not perish.

In your aloneness you have watched with our days, and in your wakefulness you have listened to the weeping and the laughter of our sleep.

Now therefore disclose us to ourselves, and tell us all that has been shown you of that which is between birth and death.

And he answered:

People of Orphalese, of what can I speak save of that which is even now moving within your souls?

CHAPTER TWO

Love

T hen said Almitra, Speak to us of Love.
And he raised his head and looked upon the people, and
there fell a stillness upon them. And with a great voice he said:
When love beckons to you, follow him,
Though his ways are hard and steep.
And when his wings enfold you yield to him,
Though the sword hidden among his pinions may
wound you.
And when he speaks to you believe in him,
Though his voice may shatter your dreams as the north
wind lays waste the garden.

For even as love crowns you so shall he crucify you. Even as
he is for your growth so is he for your pruning.
Even as he ascends to your height and caresses your
tenderest branches that quiver in the sun,
So shall he descend to your roots and shake them in their
clinging to the earth.
Like sheaves of corn he gathers you unto himself.
He threshes you to make you naked.
He sifts you to free you from your husks.
He grinds you to whiteness.
He kneads you until you are pliant;
And then he assigns you to his sacred fire, that you may
become sacred bread for God's sacred feast.

All these things shall love do unto you that you may know the secrets of your heart, and in that knowledge become a fragment of Life's heart.

But if in your fear you would seek only love's peace and love's pleasure,
Then it is better for you that you cover your nakedness and pass out of love's threshing-floor,
Into the seasonless world where you shall laugh, but not all of your laughter, and weep, but not all of your tears.

Love gives naught but itself and takes naught but from itself.
Love possesses not nor would it be possessed;
For love is sufficient unto love.

When you love you should not say, "God is in my heart," but rather, "I am in the heart of God."

And think not you can direct the course of love, for love, if it finds you worthy, directs your course.

Love has no other desire but to fulfil itself.
But if you love and must needs have desires, let these be your desires:
To melt and be like a running brook that sings its melody to the night.
To know the pain of too much tenderness.
To be wounded by your own understanding of love;
And to bleed willingly and joyfully.
To wake at dawn with a winged heart and give thanks for another day of loving;
To rest at the noon hour and meditate love's ecstasy;
To return home at eventide with gratitude;
And then to sleep with a prayer for the beloved in your heart and a song of praise upon your lips.

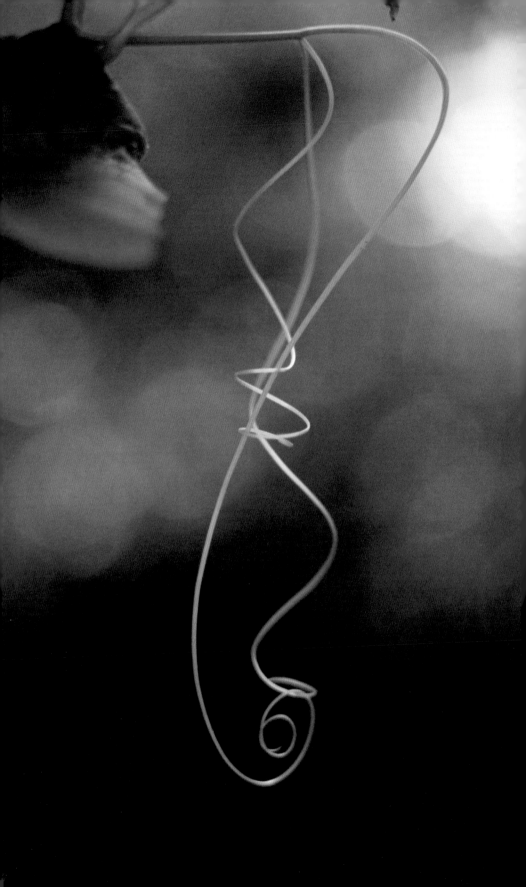

CHAPTER THREE

Marriage

Then Almitra spoke again and said,
And what of Marriage, master?
And he answered saying:
You were born together, and together you shall be
for evermore.
You shall be together when the white wings of death scatter
your days.
Aye, you shall be together even in the silent memory
of God.
But let there be spaces in your togetherness.
And let the winds of the heavens dance between you.

Love one another, but make not a bond of love:
Let it rather be a moving sea between the shores of
your souls.
Fill each other's cup but drink not from one cup.
Give one another of your bread but eat not from the
same loaf.
Sing and dance together and be joyous, but let each one of
you be alone,
Even as the strings of a lute are alone though they quiver
with the same music.

Give your hearts, but not into each other's keeping.

For only the hand of Life can contain your hearts.

And stand together yet not too near together:

For the pillars of the temple stand apart,

And the oak tree and the cypress grow not in each other's shadow.

A 12th-century underglazed ceramic from Iberia, decorated with the motif of pairs of birds in the trees.

CHAPTER FOUR

Children

And a woman who held a babe against her bosom said,
Speak to us of Children.
And he said:
Your children are not your children.
They are the sons and daughters of Life's longing for itself.
They come through you but not from you,
And though they are with you, yet they belong not to you.

You may give them your love but not your thoughts.
For they have their own thoughts.
You may house their bodies but not their souls,
For their souls dwell in the house of tomorrow, which you
cannot visit, not even in your dreams.
You may strive to be like them, but seek not to make them
like you.

For life goes not backward nor tarries with yesterday.
You are the bows from which your children as living arrows
are sent forth.

The archer sees the mark upon the path of the infinite, and
He bends you with His might that His arrows may go swift
and far.

*A 16th-century Persian manuscript illustration of everyday life in an
oasis camp with women looking after children and domestic animals.*

Let your bending in the Archer's hand be for gladness;
For even as He loves the arrow that flies, so He loves also
the bow that is stable.

*An earthenware representation of a woman feeding an infant, from
Mesopotamia, ca.2000–1800BCE.*

CHAPTER FIVE

Giving

T hen said a rich man, Speak to us of Giving.
And he answered:
You give but little when you give of your possessions.
It is when you give of yourself that you truly give.
For what are your possessions but things you keep and
guard for fear you may need them tomorrow?

And tomorrow, what shall tomorrow bring to the
overprudent dog burying bones in the trackless sand as he
follows the pilgrims to the holy city?
And what is fear of need but need itself?
Is not dread of thirst when your well is full, the thirst that
is unquenchable?
There are those who give little of the much which they have
– and they give it for recognition and their hidden desire
makes their gifts unwholesome.
And there are those who have little and give it all.
These are the believers in life and the bounty of life, and
their coffer is never empty.

There are those who give with joy, and that joy is their reward.
And there are those who give with pain, and that pain is
their baptism.

*A 6th-century floor mosaic (detail) of a fruit tree, from the Great Palace
of the Byzantine emperors in Constantinople (Istanbul).*

And there are those who give and know not pain in giving,
nor do they seek joy, nor give with mindfulness of virtue;
   They give as in yonder valley the myrtle breathes its
fragrance into space.
   Through the hands of such as these God speaks, and from
behind their eyes He smiles upon the earth.

   It is well to give when asked, but it is better to give unasked,
through understanding;
   And to the open-handed the search for one who shall
receive is joy greater than giving.
   And is there aught you would withhold?
   All you have shall some day be given;
   Therefore give now, that the season of giving may be yours
and not your inheritors'.

   You often say, "I would give, but only to the deserving."
   The trees in your orchard say not so, nor the flocks in
your pasture.
   They give that they may live, for to withhold is to perish.
   Surely he who is worthy to receive his days and his nights is
worthy of all else from you.

And he who has deserved to drink from the ocean of life deserves to fill his cup from your little stream.

And what desert greater shall there be, than that which lies in the courage and the confidence, nay the charity, of receiving?

And who are you that men should rend their bosom and unveil their pride, that you may see their worth naked and their pride unabashed?

See first that you yourself deserve to be a giver, and an instrument of giving.

For in truth it is life that gives unto life – while you, who deem yourself a giver, are but a witness.

And you receivers – and you are all receivers – assume no weight of gratitude, lest you lay a yoke upon yourself and upon him who gives.

Rather rise together with the giver on his gifts as on wings;

For to be overmindful of your debt, is to doubt his generosity who has the free-hearted earth for mother, and God for father.

CHAPTER SIX

Eating and Drinking

Then an old man, a keeper of an inn, said, Speak to us of Eating and Drinking.

And he said:

Would that you could live on the fragrance of the earth, and like an air plant be sustained by the light.

But since you must kill to eat, and rob the newly born of its mother's milk to quench your thirst, let it then be an act of worship,

And let your board stand an altar on which the pure and the innocent of forest and plain are sacrificed for that which is purer and still more innocent in man.

When you kill a beast say to him in your heart:

"By the same power that slays you, I too am slain; and I too shall be consumed.

"For the law that delivered you into my hand shall deliver me into a mightier hand.

"Your blood and my blood is naught but the sap that feeds the tree of heaven."

And when you crush an apple with your teeth, say to it in your heart:

"Your seeds shall live in my body,

A pilgrim's gilded glass bottle, flat on one side and rounded on the other, richly enamelled and decorated, from 14th-century Syria.

"And the buds of your tomorrow shall blossom in my heart,
"And your fragrance shall be my breath,
"And together we shall rejoice through all the seasons."

And in the autumn, when you gather the grapes of your vineyard for the winepress, say in your heart:
"I too am a vinyard, and my fruit shall be gathered for the winepress,
"And like new wine I shall be kept in eternal vessels."
And in winter, when you draw the wine, let there be in your heart a song for each cup;
And let there be in the song a remembrance for the autumn days, and for the vineyard, and for the winepress.

*A youth holding a cup is the main decoration on this Kubacha ware
ceramic tile, Iran, ca.1600.*

CHAPTER SEVEN

Work

Then a ploughman said, Speak to us of Work.
And he answered, saying:
You work that you may keep pace with the earth and the soul of the earth.

For to be idle is to become a stranger unto the seasons, and to step out of life's procession that marches in majesty and proud submission towards the infinite.

When you work you are a flute through whose heart the whispering of the hours turns to music.

Which of you would be a reed, dumb and silent, when all else sings together in unison?

Always you have been told that work is a curse and labour a misfortune.

But I say to you that when you work you fulfil a part of earth's furthest dream, assigned to you when that dream was born,

And in keeping yourself with labour you are in truth loving life,

And to love life through labour is to be intimate with life's inmost secret.

But if you in your pain call birth an affliction and the support of the flesh a curse written upon your brow, then I

answer that naught but the sweat of your brow shall wash
away that which is written.

You have been told also that life is darkness, and in your
weariness you echo what was said by the weary.

And I say that life is indeed darkness save when there
is urge,

And all urge is blind save when there is knowledge.

And all knowledge is vain save when there is work,

And all work is empty save when there is love;

And when you work with love you bind yourself to yourself,
and to one another, and to God.

And what is it to work with love?

It is to weave the cloth with threads drawn from your heart,
even as if your beloved were to wear that cloth.

It is to build a house with affection, even as if your beloved
were to dwell in that house.

It is to sow seeds with tenderness and reap the harvest with
joy, even as if your beloved were to eat the fruit.

It is to charge all things you fashion with a breath of your
own spirit,

And to know that all the blessed dead are standing about
you and watching.

Often have I heard you say, as if speaking in sleep,

"He who works in marble, and finds the shape of his own soul in the stone, is nobler than he who ploughs the soil.

"And he who seizes the rainbow to lay it on a cloth in the likeness of man, is more than he who makes the sandals for our feet."

But I say, not in sleep but in the over-wakefulness of noontide, that the wind speaks not more sweetly to the giant oaks than to the least of all the blades of grass;

And he alone is great who turns the voice of the wind into a song made sweeter by his own loving.

Work is love made visible.

And if you cannot work with love but only with distaste, it is better that you should leave your work and sit at the gate of the temple and take alms of those who work with joy.

For if you bake bread with indifference, you bake a bitter bread that feeds but half man's hunger.

And if you grudge the crushing of the grapes, your grudge distils a poison in the wine.

And if you sing though as angels, and love not the singing, you muffle man's ears to the voices of the day and the voices of the night.

CHAPTER EIGHT

Joy and Sorrow

Then a woman said, Speak to us of Joy and Sorrow.
And he answered:

Your joy is your sorrow unmasked.

And the selfsame well from which your laughter rises was oftentimes filled with your tears.

And how else can it be?

The deeper that sorrow carves into your being, the more joy you can contain.

Is not the cup that holds your wine the very cup that was burned in the potter's oven?

And is not the lute that soothes your spirit the very wood that was hollowed with knives?

When you are joyous, look deep into your heart and you shall find it is only that which has given you sorrow that is giving you joy.

When you are sorrowful, look again in your heart, and you shall see that in truth you are weeping for that which has been your delight.

Some of you say, "Joy is greater than sorrow," and others say, "Nay, sorrow is the greater."

But I say unto you, they are inseparable.

Contrasting red and blue floral motifs adorn an 18th-century Ottoman bath-wrap of linen embroidered with silk thread.

Together they come, and when one sits alone with you at your board, remember that the other is asleep upon your bed.

Verily you are suspended like scales between your sorrow and your joy.
Only when you are empty are you at standstill and balanced.
When the treasure-keeper lifts you to weigh his gold and his silver, needs must your joy or your sorrow rise or fall.

Predator and victim, a lion attacking a deer, form the detail in this ivory inlay from a piece of Fatimid furniture, ca. 11th century.

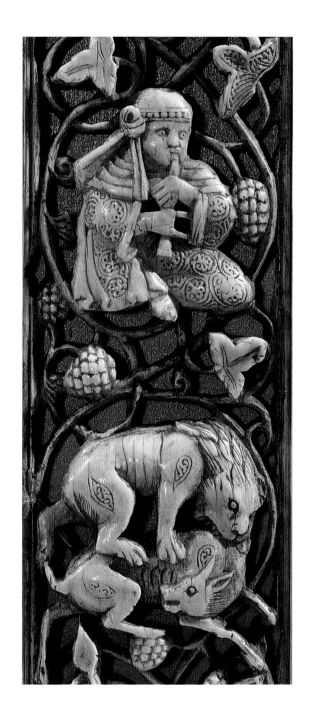

CHAPTER NINE

Houses

Then a mason came forth and said,
Speak to us of Houses.

And he answered and said:

Build of your imaginings a bower in the wilderness ere you build a house within the city walls.

For even as you have home-comings in your twilight, so has the wanderer in you, the ever-distant and alone.

Your house is your larger body.

It grows in the sun and sleeps in the stillness of the night; and it is not dreamless. Does not your house dream? And dreaming, leave the city for grove or hilltop?

Would that I could gather your houses into my hand, and like a sower scatter them in forest and meadow.

Would the valleys were your streets, and the green paths your alleys, that you might seek one another through vineyards, and come with the fragrance of the earth in your garments.

But these things are not yet to be.

In their fear your forefathers gathered you too near together. And that fear shall endure a little longer. A little longer shall your city walls separate your hearths from your fields.

And tell me, people of Orphalese, what have you in these houses? And what is it you guard with fastened doors?

Have you peace, the quiet urge that reveals your power?

Have you remembrances, the glimmering arches that span the summits of the mind?

Have you beauty, that leads the heart from things fashioned of wood and stone to the holy mountain?

Tell me, have you these in your houses?

Or have you only comfort, and the lust for comfort, that stealthy thing that enters the house a guest, and then becomes a host, and then a master?

A bulbous, lustre-painted storage vessel adorned with almond-shape medallions and "peacock's-eye" motifs. Syria, 13th century.

Ay, and it becomes a tamer, and with hook and scourge makes puppets of your larger desires.

Though its hands are silken, its heart is of iron.

It lulls you to sleep only to stand by your bed and jeer at the dignity of the flesh.

It makes mock of your sound senses, and lays them in thistledown like fragile vessels.

Verily the lust for comfort murders the passion of the soul, and then walks grinning in the funeral.

But you, children of space, you restless in rest, you shall not be trapped nor tamed.

Your house shall be not an anchor but a mast.

It shall not be a glistening film that covers a wound, but an eyelid that guards the eye.

You shall not fold your wings that you may pass through doors, nor bend your heads that they strike not against a ceiling, nor fear to breathe lest walls should crack and fall down.

You shall not dwell in tombs made by the dead for the living.

And though of magnificence and splendour, your house shall not hold your secret nor shelter your longing.

For that which is boundless in you abides in the mansion of the sky, whose door is the morning mist, and whose windows are the songs and the silences of night.

CHAPTER TEN

Clothes

And the weaver said, Speak to us of Clothes.
And he answered:

Your clothes conceal much of your beauty, yet they hide not the unbeautiful.

And though you seek in garments the freedom of privacy you may find in them a harness and a chain.

Would that you could meet the sun and the wind with more of your skin and less of your raiment.

For the breath of life is in the sunlight and the hand of life is in the wind.

Some of you say, "It is the north wind who has woven the clothes we wear."

And I say, Ay, it was the north wind,

But shame was his loom, and the softening of the sinews was his thread.

And when his work was done he laughed in the forest.

Forget not that modesty is for a shield against the eye of the unclean.

And when the unclean shall be no more, what were modesty but a fetter and a fouling of the mind?

And forget not that the earth delights to feel your bare feet and the winds long to play with your hair.

A colourful plate adorned with a figure wearing an ankle-length coat known as an entari. Anatolia, 17th century.

CHAPTER ELEVEN

Buying and Selling

A nd a merchant said, Speak to us of Buying and Selling. And he answered and said:

To you the earth yields her fruit, and you shall not want if you but know how to fill your hands.

It is in exchanging the gifts of the earth that you shall find abundance and be satisfied.

Yet unless the exchange be in love and kindly justice, it will but lead some to greed and others to hunger.

When in the marketplace you toilers of the sea and fields and vineyards meet the weavers and the potters and the gatherers of spices,–

Invoke then the master spirit of the earth, to come into your midst and sanctify the scales and the reckoning that weighs value against value.

And suffer not the barren-handed to take part in your transactions, who would sell their words for your labour.

To such men you should say,

"Come with us to the field, or go with our brothers to the sea and cast your net;

"For the land and the sea shall be bountiful to you even as to us."

The Winehouse of Anah, from a 13th-century illustrated Makamat *by* Hariri (1054–1122), *a collection of tales about a man living on his wits.*

And if there come the singers and the dancers and the flute players, – buy of their gifts also.

For they too are gatherers of fruit and frankincense, and that which they bring, though fashioned of dreams, is raiment and food for your soul.

And before you leave the marketplace, see that no one has gone his way with empty hands.

For the master spirit of the earth shall not sleep peacefully upon the wind till the needs of the least of you are satisfied.

CHAPTER TWELVE

Crime and Punishment

Then one of the judges of the city stood forth and said,
Speak to us of Crime and Punishment.

And he answered saying:

It is when your spirit goes wandering upon the wind,

That you, alone and unguarded, commit a wrong unto
others and therefore unto yourself.

And for that wrong committed must you knock and wait a
while unheeded at the gate of the blessed.

Like the ocean is your god-self;

It remains for ever undefiled.

And like the ether it lifts but the winged.

Even like the sun is your god-self;

It knows not the ways of the mole nor seeks it the holes of
the serpent.

But your god-self dwells not alone in your being.

Much in you is still man, and much in you is not yet man,

But a shapeless pigmy that walks asleep in the mist
searching for its own awakening.

And of the man in you would I now speak.

For it is he and not your god-self nor the pigmy in the mist
that knows crime and the punishment of crime.

*A late 13th-century miniature painting of guards accompanying a bound
prisoner, from Baghdad, Iraq.*

Oftentimes have I heard you speak of one who commits a wrong as though he were not one of you, but a stranger unto you and an intruder upon your world.

But I say that even as the holy and the righteous cannot rise beyond the highest which is in each one of you,

So the wicked and the weak cannot fall lower than the lowest which is in you also.

And as a single leaf turns not yellow but with the silent knowledge of the whole tree,

So the wrong-doer cannot do wrong without the hidden will of you all.

Like a procession you walk together towards your god-self.

You are the way and the wayfarers.

And when one of you falls down he falls for those behind him, a caution against the stumbling stone.

Ay, and he falls for those ahead of him, who, though faster and surer of foot, yet removed not the stumbling stone.

And this also, though the word lie heavy upon your hearts:

The murdered is not unaccountable for his own murder,

And the robbed is not blameless in being robbed.

The righteous is not innocent of the deeds of the wicked,

And the white-handed is not clean in the doings of the felon.

Yea, the guilty is oftentimes the victim of the injured,

And still more often the condemned is the burden-bearer for the guiltless and unblamed.

You cannot separate the just from the unjust and the good from the wicked;

For they stand together before the face of the sun even as the black thread and the white are woven together.

And when the black thread breaks, the weaver shall look into the whole cloth, and he shall examine the loom also.

If any of you would bring to judgment the unfaithful wife,
    Let him also weight the heart of her husband in scales, and measure his soul with measurements.
    And let him who would lash the offender look unto the spirit of the offended.
    And if any of you would punish in the name of righteousness and lay the axe unto the evil tree, let him see to its roots;
    And verily he will find the roots of the good and the bad, the fruitful and the fruitless, all entwined together in the silent heart of the earth.
    And you judges who would be just,
    What judgment pronounce you upon him who though honest in the flesh yet is a thief in spirit?
    What penalty lay you upon him who slays in the flesh yet is himself slain in the spirit?
    And how prosecute you him who in action is a deceiver and an oppressor,
    Yet who also is aggrieved and outraged?

And how shall you punish those whose remorse is already greater than their misdeeds?
    Is not remorse the justice which is administered by that very law which you would fain serve?
    Yet you cannot lay remorse upon the innocent nor lift it from the heart of the guilty.
    Unbidden shall it call in the night, that men may wake and gaze upon themselves.

And you who would understand justice, how shall you unless you look upon all deeds in the fullness of light?

Only then shall you know that the erect and the fallen are but one man standing in twilight between the night of his pigmy-self and the day of his god-self,

And that the corner-stone of the temple is not higher than the lowest stone in its foundation.

CHAPTER THIRTEEN

Laws

Then a lawyer said, But what of our Laws, master?
    And he answered:
You delight in laying down laws,
Yet you delight more in breaking them.
Like children playing by the ocean who build sand-towers
with constancy and then destroy them with laughter.
But while you build your sand-towers the ocean brings more
sand to the shore,
And when you destroy them the ocean laughs with you.
Verily the ocean laughs always with the innocent.

But what of those to whom life is not an ocean, and
man-made laws are not sand-towers,
But to whom life is a rock, and the law a chisel with which
they would carve it in their own likeness?
What of the cripple who hates dancers?
What of the ox who loves his yoke and deems the elk and
deer of the forest stray and vagrant things?
What of the old serpent who cannot shed his skin, and calls
all others naked and shameless?
And of him who comes early to the wedding-feast, and
when over-fed and tired goes his way saying that all feasts are
violation and all feasters law-breakers?

*A man puts his case before an assembly of sages. Miniature, in gouache,
late 16th century, from Boukhara, Central Asia.*

What shall I say of these save that they too stand in the sunlight, but with their backs to the sun?

They see only their shadows, and their shadows are their laws.

And what is the sun to them but a caster of shadows?

And what is it to acknowledge the laws but to stoop down and trace their shadows upon the earth?

But you who walk facing the sun, what images drawn on the earth can hold you?

You who travel with the wind, what weather-vane shall direct your course?

What man's law shall bind you if you break your yoke but upon no man's prison door?

What laws shall you fear if you dance but stumble against no man's iron chains?

And who is he that shall bring you to judgment if you tear off your garment yet leave it in no man's path?

People of Orphalese, you can muffle the drum, and you can loosen the strings of the lyre, but who shall command the skylark not to sing?

CHAPTER FOURTEEN

Freedom

A nd an orator said, Speak to us of Freedom.
And he answered:
At the city gate and by your fireside I have seen you
prostrate yourself and worship your own freedom,

Even as slaves humble themselves before a tyrant and praise
him though he slays them.

Ay, in the grove of the temple and in the shadow of the
citadel I have seen the freest among you wear their freedom
as a yoke and a handcuff.

And my heart bled within me; for you can only be free
when even the desire of seeking freedom becomes a harness
to you, and when you cease to speak of freedom as a goal and
a fulfillment.

You shall be free indeed when your days are not without a
care nor your nights without a want and a grief,

But rather when these things girdle your life and yet you
rise above them naked and unbound.

And how shall you rise beyond your days and nights
unless you break the chains which you at the dawn of your
understanding have fastened around your noon hour?

In truth that which you call freedom is the strongest of these
chains, though its links glitter in the sun and dazzle your eyes.

*Rustam, the freedom-loving Persian national hero, greets his grandfather
Sam (right), from a manuscript of the* Shahnameh, *16th century.*

And what is it but fragments of your own self you would discard that you may become free?

If it is an unjust law you would abolish, that law was written with your own hand upon your own forehead.

You cannot erase it by burning your law books nor by washing the foreheads of your judges, though you pour the sea upon them.

And if it is a despot you would dethrone, see first that his throne erected within you is destroyed.

For how can a tyrant rule the free and the proud, but for a tyranny in their own freedom and a shame in their own pride?

And if it is a care you would cast off, that care has been chosen by you rather than imposed upon you.

And if it is a fear you would dispel, the seat of that fear is in your heart and not in the hand of the feared.

Verily all things move within your being in constant half embrace, the desired and the dreaded, the repugnant and the cherished, the pursued and that which you would escape.

These things move within you as lights and shadows in pairs that cling.

And when the shadow fades and is no more, the light that lingers becomes a shadow to another light.

And thus your freedom when it loses its fetters becomes itself the fetter of a greater freedom.

CHAPTER FIFTEEN

Reason and Passion

And the priestess spoke again and said:
Speak to us of Reason and Passion.

And he answered saying:

Your soul is oftentimes a battlefield, upon which your reason and your judgment wage war against passion and your appetite.

Would that I could be the peacemaker in your soul, that I might turn the discord and the rivalry of your elements into oneness and melody.

But how shall I, unless you yourselves be also the peacemakers, nay, the lovers of all your elements?

Your reason and your passion are the rudder and the sails of your seafaring soul.

If either your sails or your rudder be broken, you can but toss and drift, or else be held at a standstill in mid-seas.

For reason, ruling alone, is a force confining; and passion, unattended, is a flame that burns to its own destruction.

Therefore let your soul exalt your reason to the height of passion, that it may sing;

And let it direct your passion with reason, that your passion may live through its own daily resurrection, and like the phoenix rise above its own ashes.

I would have you consider your judgment and your appetite even as you would two loved guests in your house.

An early 15th-century woollen carpet decorated with a design based on a phoenix and an elemental dragon.

Surely you would not honour one guest above the other; for he who is more mindful of one loses the love and the faith of both.

Among the hills, when you sit in the cool shade of the white poplars, sharing the peace and serenity of distant fields and meadows – then let your heart say in silence, "God rests in reason."

And when the storm comes, and the mighty wind shakes the forest, and thunder and lightning proclaim the majesty of the sky, – then let your heart say in awe, "God moves in passion."

And since you are a breath in God's sphere, and a leaf in God's forest, you too should rest in reason and move in passion.

CHAPTER SIXTEEN

Pain

A nd a woman spoke, saying, Tell us of Pain.
  And he said:

Your pain is the breaking of the shell that encloses your understanding.

Even as the stone of the fruit must break, that its heart may stand in the sun, so must you know pain.

And could you keep your heart in wonder at the daily miracles of your life, your pain would not seem less wondrous than your joy;

And you would accept the seasons of your heart, even as you have always accepted the seasons that pass over your fields.

And you would watch with serenity through the winters of your grief.

Much of your pain is self-chosen.

It is the bitter potion by which the physician within you heals your sick self.

A carved ivory plaque (detail), from a piece of furniture, shows a grim-faced participant at the feast, ca. 11th–12th century.

Therefore trust the physician, and drink his remedy in silence and tranquillity:

For his hand, though heavy and hard, is guided by the tender hand of the Unseen,

And the cup he brings, though it burn your lips, has been fashioned of the clay which the Potter has moistened with His own sacred tears.

*Competing horsemen adorn a 12th–13th-century painted earthenware
pot from Iran.*

CHAPTER SEVENTEEN

Self-Knowledge

And a man said, Speak to us of Self-Knowledge.

And he answered, saying:

Your hearts know in silence the secrets of the days and the nights.

But your ears thirst for the sound of your heart's knowledge.

You would know in words that which you have always known in thought.

You would touch with your fingers the naked body of your dreams.

And it is well you should.

The hidden well-spring of your soul must needs rise and run murmuring to the sea;

And the treasure of your infinite depths would be revealed to your eyes.

But let there be no scales to weigh your unknown treasure;

And seek not the depths of your knowledge with staff or sounding line.

For self is a sea boundless and measureless.

Say not, "I have found the truth," but rather, "I have found a truth."

Say not, "I have found the path of the soul." Say rather,
"I have met the soul walking upon my path."

For the soul walks upon all paths.

The soul walks not upon a line, neither does it grow like
a reed.

The soul unfolds itself, like a lotus of countless petals.

*Two ivory plaques with palmettes and lotus leaves, decorated in
Phoenician style, ca. 13th century* BCE

CHAPTER EIGHTEEN

Teaching

T hen said a teacher, Speak to us of Teaching.
And he said:

No man can reveal to you aught but that which already lies half asleep in the dawning of your knowledge.

The teacher who walks in the shadow of the temple, among his followers, gives not of his wisdom but rather of his faith and his lovingness.

If he is indeed wise he does not bid you enter the house of his wisdom, but rather leads you to the threshold of your own mind.

The astronomer may speak to you of his understanding of space, but he cannot give you his understanding.

The musician may sing to you of the rhythm which is in all space, but he cannot give you the ear which arrests the rhythm, nor the voice that echoes it.

And he who is versed in the science of numbers can tell of the regions of weight and measure, but he cannot conduct you thither.

For the vision of one man lends not its wings to another man.

And even as each one of you stands alone in God's knowledge, so must each one of you be alone in his knowledge of God and in his understanding of the earth.

Two Indian astronomers observe the stars, from a Sanskrit astrological treatise, ca. 1840.

CHAPTER NINETEEN

Friendship

And a youth said, Speak to us of Friendship.
And he answered, saying:

Your friend is your needs answered.

He is your field which you sow with love and reap with thanksgiving.

And he is your board and your fireside.

For you come to him with your hunger, and you seek him for peace.

When your friend speaks his mind you fear not the "nay" in your own mind, nor do you withhold the "ay."

And when he is silent your heart ceases not to listen to his heart;

For without words, in friendship, all thoughts, all desires, all expectations are born and shared, with joy that is unacclaimed.

When you part from your friend, you grieve not;

For that which you love most in him may be clearer in his absence, as the mountain to the climber is clearer from the plain.

And let there be no purpose in friendship save the deepening of the spirit.

For love that seeks aught but the disclosure of its own mystery is not love but a net cast forth: and only the unprofitable is caught.

And let your best be for your friend.

If he must know the ebb of your tide, let him know its flood also.

For what is your friend that you should seek him with hours to kill?

Seek him always with hours to live.

For it is his to fill your need, but not your emptiness.

And in the sweetness of friendship let there be laughter, and sharing of pleasures.

For in the dew of little things the heart finds its morning and is refreshed.

Glazed terracotta plate showing two men relaxing near a stream,
18th-century Iran.

CHAPTER TWENTY

Talking

And then a scholar said, Speak of Talking.

And he answered, saying:

You talk when you cease to be at peace with your thoughts;

And when you can no longer dwell in the solitude of your heart you live in your lips, and sound is a diversion and a pastime.

And in much of your talking, thinking is half murdered.

For thought is a bird of space, that in a cage of words may indeed unfold its wings but cannot fly.

There are those among you who seek the talkative through fear of being alone.

The silence of aloneness reveals to their eyes their naked selves and they would escape.

And there are those who talk, and without knowledge or forethought reveal a truth which they themselves do not understand.

And there are those who have the truth within them, but they tell it not in words.

In the bosom of such as these the spirit dwells in rhythmic silence.

A 16th-century Ottoman plate, from Iznik, showing the king being petitioned, from Firdausi's Shahnameh *(Book of Kings).*

When you meet your friend on the roadside or in the market-place, let the spirit in you move your lips and direct your tongue.

Let the voice within your voice speak to the ear of his ear;

For his soul will keep the truth of your heart as the taste of the wine is remembered

When the colour is forgotten and the vessel is no more.

A bird at rest in the bough of a tree, a colourful Ottoman ceramic from Iznik, 16th century.

CHAPTER TWENTY-ONE

Time

And an astronomer said, Master, what of Time?
And he answered:

You would measure time the measureless and the immeasurable.

You would adjust your conduct and even direct the course of your spirit according to hours and seasons.

Of time you would make a stream upon whose bank you would sit and watch its flowing.

Yet the timeless in you is aware of life's timelessness,

And knows that yesterday is but today's memory and tomorrow is today's dream.

And that that which sings and contemplates in you is still dwelling within the bounds of that first moment which scattered the stars into space.

Who among you does not feel that his power to love is boundless?

And yet who does not feel that very love, though boundless, encompassed within the centre of his being, and moving not from love thought to love thought, nor from love deeds to other love deeds?

And is not time even as love is, undivided and paceless?

But if in your thought you must measure time into seasons, let each season encircle all the other seasons,

And let today embrace the past with remembrance and the future with longing.

CHAPTER TWENTY-TWO

Good and Evil

And one of the elders of the city said, Speak to us of Good and Evil.

And he answered:

Of the good in you I can speak, but not of the evil.

For what is evil but good tortured by its own hunger and thirst?

Verily when good is hungry it seeks food even in dark caves, and when it thirsts, it drinks even of dead waters.

You are good when you are one with yourself.

Yet when you are not one with yourself you are not evil.

For a divided house is not a den of thieves; it is only a divided house.

And a ship without rudder may wander aimlessly among perilous isles yet sink not to the bottom.

You are good when you strive to give of yourself.

Yet you are not evil when you seek gain for yourself.

For when you strive for gain you are but a root that clings to the earth and sucks at her breast.

Surely the fruit cannot say to the root, "Be like me, ripe and full and ever giving of your abundance."

For to the fruit giving is a need, as receiving is a need to the root.

You are good when you are fully awake in your speech,
Yet you are not evil when you sleep while your tongue
staggers without purpose.
And even stumbling speech may strengthen a weak tongue.

You are good when you walk to your goal firmly and with
bold steps.
Yet you are not evil when you go thither limping.
Even those who limp go not backward.
But you who are strong and swift, see that you do not limp
before the lame, deeming it kindness.

You are good in countless ways, and you are not evil when
you are not good,
You are only loitering and sluggard.
Pity that the stags cannot teach swiftness to the turtles.

In your longing for your giant self lies your goodness: and that longing is in all of you.

But in some of you that longing is a torrent rushing with might to the sea, carrying the secrets of the hillsides and the songs of the forest.

And in others it is a flat stream that loses itself in angles and bends and lingers before it reaches the shore.

But let not him who longs much say to him who longs little, "Wherefore are you slow and halting?"

For the truly good ask not the naked, "Where is your garment?" nor the houseless, "What has befallen your house?"

Deer bounding swiftly away from danger embellish a 17th-century silk cloth from Safavid Iran.

CHAPTER TWENTY-THREE

Prayer

Then a Priestess said, Speak to us of Prayer.
And he answered, saying:
You pray in your distress and in your need; would that you might pray also in the fullness of your joy and in your days of abundance.

For what is prayer but the expansion of yourself into the living ether?

And if it is for your comfort to pour your darkness into space, it is also for your delight to pour forth the dawning of your heart.

And if you cannot but weep when your soul summons you to prayer, she should spur you again and yet again, though weeping, until you shall come laughing.

When you pray you rise to meet in the air those who are praying at that very hour, and whom save in prayer you may not meet.

Therefore let your visit to that temple invisible be for naught but ecstasy and sweet communion.

For if you should enter the temple for no other purpose than asking you shall not receive:

And if you should enter into it to humble yourself you shall not be lifted:

Or even if you should enter into it to beg for the good of others you shall not be heard.

It is enough that you enter the temple invisible.

I cannot teach you how to pray in words.

God listens not to your words save when He Himself utters them through your lips.

And I cannot teach you the prayer of the seas and the forests and the mountains.

But you who are born of the mountains and the forests and the seas can find their prayer in your heart,

And if you but listen in the stillness of the night you shall hear them saying in silence:

"Our God, who art our winged self, it is thy will in us that willeth.

"It is thy desire in us that desireth.

"It is thy urge in us that would turn our nights, which are thine, into days which are thine also.

"We cannot ask thee for aught, for thou knowest our needs before they are born in us:

"Thou art our need; and in giving us more of thyself thou givest us all."

CHAPTER TWENTY-FOUR

Pleasure

Then a hermit, who visited the city once a year, came forth and said, Speak to us of Pleasure.

And he answered, saying:

Pleasure is a freedom-song,

But it is not freedom.

It is the blossoming of your desires,

But it is not their fruit.

It is a depth calling unto a height,

But it is not the deep nor the high.

It is the caged taking wing,

But it is not space encompassed.

Ay, in very truth, pleasure is a freedom-song.

And I fain would have you sing it with fullness of heart; yet I would not have you lose your hearts in the singing.

Some of your youth seek pleasure as if it were all, and they are judged and rebuked.

I would not judge nor rebuke them. I would have them seek.

For they shall find pleasure, but not her alone:

Seven are her sisters, and the least of them is more beautiful than pleasure.

Have you not heard of the man who was digging in the earth for roots and found a treasure?

And some of your elders remember pleasures with regret like wrongs committed in drunkenness.

But regret is the beclouding of the mind and not its chastisement.

They should remember their pleasures with gratitude, as they would the harvest of a summer.

Yet if it comforts them to regret, let them be comforted.

And there are among you those who are neither young to seek nor old to remember;

And in their fear of seeking and remembering they shun all pleasures, lest they neglect the spirit or offend against it.

But even in their foregoing is their pleasure.

And thus they too find a treasure though they dig for roots with quivering hands.

But tell me, who is he that can offend the spirit?

Shall the nightingale offend the stillness of the night, or the firefly the stars?

And shall your flame or your smoke burden the wind?

Think you the spirit is a still pool which you can trouble with a staff?

Oftentimes in denying yourself pleasure you do but store the desire in the recesses of your being.

Who knows but that which seems omitted today, waits for tomorrow?

Even your body knows its heritage and its rightful need and will not be deceived.

And your body is the harp of your soul,

And it is yours to bring forth sweet music from it or confused sounds.

And now you ask in your heart, "How shall we distinguish that which is good in pleasure from that which is not good?"

Go to your fields and your gardens, and you shall learn that it is the pleasure of the bee to gather honey of the flower,

But it is also the pleasure of the flower to yield its honey to the bee.

For to the bee a flower is a fountain of life,

And to the flower a bee is a messenger of love,

And to both, bee and flower, the giving and the receiving of pleasure is a need and an ecstasy.

People of Orphalese, be in your pleasures like the flowers and the bees.

CHAPTER TWENTY-FIVE

Beauty

And a poet said, Speak to us of Beauty.
And he answered:

Where shall you seek beauty, and how shall you find her
unless she herself be your way and your guide?

And how shall you speak of her except she be the weaver
of your speech?

The aggrieved and the injured say, "Beauty is kind
and gentle.

"Like a young mother half-shy of her own glory she walks
among us."

And the passionate say, "Nay, beauty is a thing of might
and dread.

"Like the tempest she shakes the earth beneath us and the
sky above us."

The tired and the weary say, "Beauty is of soft whisperings.
She speaks in our spirit.

"Her voice yields to our silences like a faint light that
quivers in fear of the shadow."

But the restless say, "We have heard her shouting among the
mountains,

---

*A handsome youth holds a flask and drinks from a cup in a vibrant
Safavid silk cloth design by Rizzi-i-Abbasi, 17th century.*

"And with her cries came the sound of hoofs, and the beating of wings and the roaring of lions."

At night the watchmen of the city say, "Beauty shall rise with the dawn from the east."
And at noontide the toilers and the wayfarers say, "We have seen her leaning over the earth from the windows of the sunset."

In winter say the snow-bound, "She shall come with the spring leaping upon the hills."
And in the summer heat the reapers say, "We have seen her dancing with the autumn leaves, and we saw a drift of snow in her hair."
All these things have you said of beauty,
Yet in truth you spoke not of her but of needs unsatisfied,
And beauty is not a need but an ecstasy.

It is not a mouth thirsting nor an empty hand
stretched forth,
But rather a heart inflamed and a soul enchanted.
It is not the image you would see nor the song you
would hear,
But rather an image you see though you close your eyes and
a song you hear though you shut your ears.
It is not the sap within the furrowed bark, nor a wing
attached to a claw,
But rather a garden for ever in bloom and a flock of angels
for ever in flight.

People of Orphalese, beauty is life when life unveils her
holy face.
But you are life and you are the veil.
Beauty is eternity gazing at itself in a mirror.
But you are eternity and you are the mirror.

CHAPTER TWENTY-SIX

Religion

And an old priest said, Speak to us of Religion.
And he said:

Have I spoken this day of aught else?

Is not religion all deeds and all reflection,

And that which is neither deed nor reflection, but a wonder and a surprise ever springing in the soul, even while the hands hew the stone or tend the loom?

Who can separate his faith from his actions, or his belief from his occupations?

Who can spread his hours before him, saying, "This for God and this for myself; This for my soul, and this other for my body"?

All your hours are wings that beat through space from self to self.

He who wears his morality but as his best garment were better naked.

The wind and the sun will tear no holes in his skin.

And he who defines his conduct by ethics imprisons his song-bird in a cage.

The freest song comes not through bars and wires.

And he to whom worshipping is a window, to open but also to shut, has not yet visited the house of his soul whose windows are from dawn to dawn.

Your daily life is your temple and your religion.
Whenever you enter into it take with you your all.
Take the plough and the forge and the mallet and the lute,
The things you have fashioned in necessity or for delight.
For in reverie you cannot rise above your achievements nor
fall lower than your failures.
And take with you all men:
For in adoration you cannot fly higher than their hopes nor
humble yourself lower than their despair.

And if you would know God, be not therefore a solver
of riddles.
Rather look about you and you shall see Him playing with
your children.
And look into space; you shall see Him walking in the
cloud, outstretching His arms in the lightning and
descending in rain.
You shall see Him smiling in flowers, then rising and waving
His hands in trees.

CHAPTER TWENTY-SEVEN

Death

Then Almitra spoke, saying, We would ask now
of Death.

And he said:

You would know the secret of death.

But how shall you find it unless you seek it in the heart
of life?

The owl whose night-bound eyes are blind unto the day
cannot unveil the mystery of light.

If you would indeed behold the spirit of death, open your
heart wide unto the body of life.

For life and death are one, even as the river and the sea
are one.

In the depth of your hopes and desires lies your silent
knowledge of the beyond;

And like seeds dreaming beneath the snow your heart
dreams of spring.

Trust the dreams, for in them is hidden the gate to eternity.

Your fear of death is but the trembling of the shepherd
when he stands before the king whose hand is to be laid upon
him in honour.

Is the shepherd not joyful beneath his trembling, that he
shall wear the mark of the king?

---

*An angel of death from a 16th-century Iranian miniature – non-terrifying
in appearance, this angel has come for the soul of a good person.*

Yet is he not more mindful of his trembling?

For what is it to die but to stand naked in the wind and to melt into the sun?
And what is it to cease breathing but to free the breath from its restless tides, that it may rise and expand and seek God unencumbered?

Only when you drink from the river of silence shall you indeed sing.
And when you have reached the mountain top, then you shall begin to climb.
And when the earth shall claim your limbs, then shall you truly dance.

Attendants surround a king sitting on his throne, in a garden, while he greets a visitor. Enamelled ceramic, Kashan, Iran, late 12th century.

CHAPTER TWENTY-EIGHT

The Farewell

And now it was evening.

And Almitra the seeress said, Blessed be this day and this place and your spirit that has spoken.

And he answered, Was it I who spoke?

Was I not also a listener?

Then he descended the steps of the Temple and all the people followed him. And he reached his ship and stood upon the deck.

And facing the people again, he raised his voice and said:

People of Orphalese, the wind bids me leave you.

Less hasty am I than the wind, yet I must go.

We wanderers, ever seeking the lonelier way, begin no day where we have ended another day; and no sunrise finds us where sunset left us.

Even while the earth sleeps we travel.

We are the seeds of the tenacious plant, and it is in our ripeness and our fullness of heart that we are given to the wind and are scattered.

Brief were my days among you, and briefer still the words I have spoken.

But should my voice fade in your ears, and my love vanish in your memory, then I will come again,

And with a richer heart and lips more yielding to the spirit will I speak.

Yea, I shall return with the tide,

And though death may hide me, and the greater silence
enfold me, yet again will I seek your understanding.

And not in vain will I seek.

If aught I have said is truth, that truth shall reveal itself in a
clearer voice, and in words more kin to your thoughts.

I go with the wind, people of Orphalese, but not down into
emptiness;

And if this day is not a fulfilment of your needs and my
love, then let it be a promise till another day.

Man's needs change, but not his love, nor his desire that his
love should satisfy his needs.

Know, therefore, that from the greater silence I shall return.

The mist that drifts away at dawn, leaving but dew in the
fields, shall rise and gather into a cloud and then fall down
in rain.

And not unlike the mist have I been.

In the stillness of the night I have walked in your streets,
and my spirit has entered your houses,

And your heart-beats were in my heart, and your breath was
upon my face, and I knew you all.

Ay, I knew your joy and your pain, and in your sleep your
dreams were my dreams.

And oftentimes I was among you a lake among the mountains.

I mirrored the summits in you and the bending slopes, and
even the passing flocks of your thoughts and your desires.

And to my silence came the laughter of your children in
streams, and the longing of your youths in rivers.

And when they reached my depth the streams and the rivers
ceased not yet to sing.

But sweeter still than laughter and greater than longing
came to me.
   It was boundless in you;
   The vast man in whom you are all but cells and sinews;
   He in whose chant all your singing is but a soundless
throbbing.
   It is in the vast man that you are vast,
   And in beholding him that I beheld you and loved you.
   For what distances can love reach that are not in that
vast sphere?
   What visions, what expectations and what presumptions
can outsoar that flight?
   Like a giant oak tree covered with apple blossoms is the vast
man in you.
   His might binds you to the earth, his fragrance lifts you into
space, and in his durability you are deathless.

   You have been told that, even like a chain, you are as weak
as your weakest link.
   This is but half the truth. You are also as strong as your
strongest link.
   To measure you by your smallest deed is to reckon the
power of ocean by the frailty of its foam.
   To judge you by your failures is to cast blame upon the
seasons for their inconsistency.

   Ay, you are like an ocean,
   And though heavy-grounded ships await the tide upon your
shores, yet, even like an ocean, you cannot hasten your tides.
   And like the seasons you are also,
   And though in your winter you deny your spring,

Yet spring, reposing within you, smiles in her drowsiness and is not offended.

Think not I say these things in order that you may say the one to the other, "He praised us well. He saw but the good in us."

I only speak to you in words of that which you yourselves know in thought.

And what is word knowledge but a shadow of wordless knowledge?

Your thoughts and my words are waves from a sealed memory that keeps records of our yesterdays,

And of the ancient days when the earth knew not us nor herself,

And of nights when earth was upwrought with confusion.

Wise men have come to you to give you of their wisdom. I came to take of your wisdom:

And behold I have found that which is greater than wisdom.

It is a flame spirit in you ever gathering more of itself,

While you, heedless of its expansion, bewail the withering of your days.

It is life in quest of life in bodies that fear the grave.

There are no graves here.

These mountains and plains are a cradle and a stepping-stone.

Whenever you pass by the field where you have laid your ancestors look well thereupon, and you shall see yourselves and your children dancing hand in hand.

Verily you often make merry without knowing.

*An earthenware tin-glazed, lustre-painted bowl decorated with an
ocean-going vessel. Valencia or Málaga, ca.1300.*

Others have come to you to whom for golden promises made unto your faith you have given but riches and power and glory.

Less than a promise have I given, and yet more generous have you been to me.

You have given me deeper thirsting after life.

Surely there is no greater gift to a man than that which turns all his aims into parching lips and all life into a fountain.

And in this lies my honour and my reward, –

That whenever I come to the fountain to drink I find the living water itself thirsty;

And it drinks me while I drink it.

Some of you have deemed me proud and over-shy to receive gifts.

Too proud indeed am I to receive wages, but not gifts.

And though I have eaten berries among the hill when you would have had me sit at your board,

And slept in the portico of the temple when you would gladly have sheltered me,

Yet was it not your loving mindfulness of my days and my nights that made food sweet to my mouth and girdled my sleep with visions?

For this I bless you most:

You give much and know not that you give at all.

Verily the kindness that gazes upon itself in a mirror turns to stone,

And a good deed that calls itself by tender names becomes the parent to a curse.

And some of you have called me aloof, and drunk with my own aloneness,

And you have said, "He holds council with the trees of the forest, but not with men.

"He sits alone on hill-tops and looks down upon our city."

True it is that I have climbed the hills and walked in remote places.

How could I have seen you save from a great height or a great distance?

How can one be indeed near unless he be far?

And others among you called unto me, not in words, and they said:

"Stranger, stranger, lover of unreachable heights, why dwell you among the summits where eagles build their nests?

"Why seek you the unattainable?

"What storms would you trap in your net,

"And what vaporous birds do you hunt in the sky?

"Come and be one of us.

"Descend and appease your hunger with our bread and quench your thirst with our wine."

In the solitude of their souls they said these things;

But were their solitude deeper they would have known that I sought but the secret of your joy and your pain,

And I hunted only your larger selves that walk the sky.

But the hunter was also the hunted:

For many of my arrows left my bow only to seek my own breast.

And the flier was also the creeper;

For when my wings were spread in the sun their shadow upon the earth was a turtle.

And I the believer was also the doubter;

For often have I put my finger in my own wound that I might have the greater belief in you and the greater knowledge of you.

And it is with this belief and this knowledge that I say,

You are not enclosed within your bodies, nor confined to houses or fields.

That which is you dwells above the mountain and roves with the wind.

It is not a thing that crawls into the sun for warmth or digs holes into darkness for safety,

But a thing free, a spirit that envelops the earth and moves in the ether.

If this be vague words, then seek not to clear them.

Vague and nebulous is the beginning of all things, but not their end,

And I fain would have you remember me as a beginning.

Life, and all that lives, is conceived in the mist and not in the crystal.

And who knows but a crystal is mist in decay?

This would I have you remember in remembering me:

That which seems most feeble and bewildered in you is the strongest and most determined.

Is it not your breath that has erected and hardened the structure of your bones?

And is it not a dream which none of you remember having

dreamt, that builded your city and fashioned all there is in it?

   Could you but see the tides of that breath you would cease
to see all else,

   And if you could hear the whispering of the dream you
would hear no other sound.

   But you do not see, nor do you hear, and it is well.

   The veil that clouds your eyes shall be lifted by the hands
that wove it,

   And the clay that fills your ears shall be pierced by those
fingers that kneaded it.

   And you shall see

   And you shall hear.

   Yet you shall not deplore having known blindness, nor
regret having been deaf.

   For in that day you shall know the hidden purposes in
all things,

   And you shall bless darkness as you would bless light.

   After saying these things he looked about him, and he saw
the pilot of his ship standing by the helm and gazing now at
the full sails and now at the distance.

   And he said:

   Patient, over-patient, is the captain of my ship.

   The wind blows, and restless are the sails;

   Even the rudder begs direction;

   Yet quietly my captain awaits my silence.

   And these my mariners, who have heard the choir of the
greater sea, they too have heard me patiently.

Now they shall wait no longer.

I am ready.

The stream has reached the sea, and once more the great mother holds her son against her breast.

Fare you well, people of Orphalese.

This day has ended.

It is closing upon us even as the water-lily upon its own tomorrow.

What was given us here we shall keep,

And if it suffices not, then again must we come together and together stretch our hands unto the giver.

Forget not that I shall come back to you.

A little while, and my longing shall gather dust and foam for another body.

A little while, a moment of rest upon the wind, and another woman shall bear me.

Farewell to you and the youth I have spent with you.

It was but yesterday we met in a dream.

You have sung to me in my aloneness, and I of your longings have built a tower in the sky.

But now our sleep has fled and our dream is over, and it is no longer dawn.

The noontide is upon us and our half waking has turned to fuller day, and we must part.

If in the twilight of memory we should meet once more, we shall speak again together and you shall sing to me a deeper song.

And if our hands should meet in another dream we shall build another tower in the sky.

So saying he made a signal to the seamen, and straightaway they weighed anchor and cast the ship loose from its moorings, and they moved eastward.

And a cry came from the people as from a single heart, and it rose into the dusk and was carried out over the sea like a great trumpeting.

Only Almitra was silent, gazing after the ship until it had vanished into the mist.

And when all the people were dispersed she still stood alone upon the sea-wall, remembering in her heart his saying:

"A little while, a moment of rest upon the wind, and another woman shall bear me."

PART TWO

The Garden
of the Prophet

Contents

A homecoming 153

The garden of his mother and father 158

Pity the nation 159

When spring comes 161

A secret road 163

The womb of Time 165

We are all parasites 167

Light of all the years 169

Alone 170

You and the stone are one 171

We are God 172

Only the naked live in the sun 175

What is it to *be?* 176

Heavy-laden is my soul 179

Karima 183

O Mist, my sister 188

The Garden of the Prophet

Almustafa, the chosen and the beloved, who was a noon
unto his own day, returned to the isle of his birth in the
month of Tichreen, which is the month of remembrance.

And as his ship approached the harbour, he stood upon
its prow, and his mariners were about him. And there was a
homecoming in his heart.

And he spoke, and the sea was in his voice, and he said:
"Behold, the isle of our birth. Even here the earth heaved us,
a song and a riddle; a song unto the sky, a riddle unto the
earth; and what is there between earth and sky that shall
carry the song and solve the riddle save our own passion?

"The sea yields us once more to these shores. We are but
another wave of her waves. She sends us forth to sound her
speech, but how shall we do so unless we break the symmetry
of our heart on rock and sand?

"For this is the law of mariners and the sea: If you would
freedom, you must needs turn to mist. The formless is for
ever seeking form, even as the countless nebulae would
become suns and moons; and we who have sought much and
return now to this isle, rigid moulds, we must become mist
once more and learn of the beginning. And what is there that

A paradisial garden teeming with flora and fauna is woven into this
16th-century carpet from northwestern Iran.

shall live and rise unto the heights except it be broken unto passion and freedom?

"For ever shall we be in quest of the shores, that we may sing and be heard. But what of the wave that breaks where no ear shall hear? It is the unheard in us that nurses our deeper sorrow. Yet it is also the unheard which carves our soul to form and fashions our destiny."

Then one of his mariners came forth and said: "Master, you have captained our longing for this harbour, and behold, we have come. Yet you speak of sorrow, and of hearts that shall be broken."

And he answered him and said: "Did I not speak of freedom, and of the mist which is our greater freedom? Yet it is in pain I make pilgrimage to the isle where I was born, even like unto a ghost of one slain come to kneel before those who have slain him."

And another mariner spoke and said: "Behold, the multitudes on the sea-wall. In their silence they have foretold even the day and the hour of your coming, and they have gathered from their fields and vineyards in their loving need, to await you."

And Almustafa looked afar upon the multitudes, and his heart was mindful of their yearning, and he was silent.

Then a cry came from the people, and it was a cry of remembrance and of entreaty.

And he looked upon his mariners and said: "And what have I brought them? A hunter was I, in a distant land. With aim and might I have spent the golden arrows they gave me, but I have brought down no game. I followed not the arrows. Mayhap they are spreading now in the sun with the pinions of wounded eagles that would not fall to earth. And mayhap the arrow-heads have fallen into the hands of those who had need of them for bread and wine.

"I know not where they have spent their flight, but this I know: they have made their curve in the sky.

"Even so, love's hand is still upon me, and you, my mariners, still sail my vision, and I shall not be dumb. I shall cry out when the hand of the seasons is upon my throat, and I shall sing my words when my lips are burned with flames."

And they were troubled in their hearts because he spoke these things. And one said: "Master, teach us all, and mayhap because your blood flows in our veins, and our breath is of your fragrance, we shall understand."

Then he answered them, and the wind was in his voice, and he said: "Brought you me to the isle of my birth to be a teacher? Not yet have I been caged by wisdom. Too young am I and too verdant to speak of aught but self, which is for ever the deep calling upon the deep.

"Let him who would have wisdom seek it in the buttercup or in a pinch of red clay. I am still the singer. Still I shall sing the earth, and I shall sing your lost dreaming that walks the day between sleep and sleep. But I shall gaze upon the sea."

And now the ship entered the harbour and reached the sea-wall, and he came thus to the isle of his birth and stood once more amongst his own people. And a great cry arose from their hearts so that the loneliness of his homecoming was shaken within him.

And they were silent awaiting his word, but he answered them not, for the sadness of memory was upon him, and he said in his heart: "Have I said that I shall sing? Nay, I can but open my lips that the voice of life may come forth and go out to the wind for joy and support."

Then Karima, she who had played with him, a child, in the Garden of his mother, spoke and said: "Twelve years have you hidden your face from us, and for twelve years have we hungered and thirsted for your voice."

And he looked upon her with exceeding tenderness, for it was she who had closed the eyes of his mother when the white wings of death had gathered her.

And he answered and said: "Twelve years? Said you twelve years, Karima? I measured not my longing with the starry rod, nor did I sound the depth thereof. For love when love is homesick exhausts time's measurements and time's soundings.

"There are moments that hold aeons of separation. Yet parting is naught but an exhaustion of the mind. Perhaps we have not parted."

And Almustafa looked upon the people, and he saw them all, the youth and the aged, the stalwart and the puny, those also who were ruddy with the touch of wind and sun, and those who were of pallid countenance; and upon their face a light of longing and of questioning.

And one spoke and said: "Master, life has dealt bitterly with our hopes and our desires. Our hearts are troubled, and we do not understand. I pray you, comfort us, and open to us the meanings of our sorrows."

And his heart was moved with compassion, and he said: "Life is older than all things living; even as beauty was wingèd ere the beautiful was born on earth, and even as truth was truth ere it was uttered.

"Life sings in our silences, and dreams in our slumber. Even when we are beaten and low. Life is enthroned and high. And when we weep, Life smiles upon the day, and is free even when we drag our chains.

"Oftentimes we call Life bitter names, but only when we ourselves are bitter and dark. And we deem her empty and unprofitable, but only when the soul goes wandering in desolate places, and the heart is drunken with overmindfulness of self.

"Life is deep and high and distant; and though only your vast vision can reach even her feet, yet she is near; and though only the breath of your breath reaches her heart, the shadow of your shadow crosses her face, and the echo of your faintest cry becomes a spring and an autumn in her breast.

A ceramic decorated with a scene of a banquet with musicians and dancers at the court of Shah Nasser Ed-Din, mid-19th century, Iran.

"And Life is veiled and hidden, even as your greater self is hidden and veiled. Yet when Life speaks, all the winds become words; and when she speaks again, the smiles upon your lips and the tears in your eyes turn also into words. When she sings, the deaf hear and are held; and when she comes walking, the sightless behold her and are amazed and follow her in wonder and astonishment."

And he ceased from speaking, and a vast silence enfolded the people, and in the silence there was an unheard song, and they were comforted of their loneliness and their aching.

And he left them straightway and followed the path which led to his Garden, which was the Garden of his mother and his father, wherein they lay asleep, they and their forefathers.

And there were those who would have followed after him, seeing that it was a homecoming, and he was alone, for there was not one left of all his kin to spread the feast of welcome, after the manner of his people.

But the captain of his ship counselled them saying: "Suffer him to go upon his way. For his bread is the bread of aloneness, and in his cup is the wine of remembrance, which he would drink alone."

And his mariners held their steps, for they knew it was even as the captain of the ship had told them. And all those who gathered upon the sea-wall restrained the feet of their desire.

Only Karima went after him, a little way, yearning over his aloneness and his memories. And she spoke not, but turned and went unto her own house, and in the garden under the almond-tree she wept, yet knew not wherefore.

And Almustafa came and found the Garden of his mother and his father, and he entered in, and closed the gate that no man might come after him.

And for forty days and forty nights he dwelt alone in that house and that Garden, and none came, not even unto the gate, for it was closed, and all the people knew that he would be alone.

And when the forty days and nights were ended, Almustafa opened the gate that they might come in.

And there came nine men to be with him in the Garden; three mariners from his own ship; three who had served in the Temple; and three who had been his comrades in play when they were but children together. And these were his disciples.

And on a morning his disciples sat around him, and there were distances and remembrances in his eyes. And that disciple who was called Hafiz said unto him: "Master, tell us of the city of Orphalese, and of that land wherein you tarried those twelve years."

And Almustafa was silent, and he looked away towards the hills and toward the vast ether, and there was a battle in his silence.

Then he said: "My friends and my road-fellows, pity the nation that is full of beliefs and empty of religion.

"Pity the nation that wears a cloth it does not weave, eats a bread it does not harvest, and drinks a wine that flows not from its own winepress.

"Pity the nation that acclaims the bully as hero, and that deems the glittering conqueror bountiful.

"Pity the nation that despises a passion in its dream, yet submits in its awakening.

"Pity the nation that raises not its voice save when it walks in a funeral, boasts not except among its ruins, and will rebel not save when its neck is laid between the sword and the block.

"Pity the nation whose statesman is a fox, whose philosopher is a juggler, and whose art is the art of patching and mimicking.

"Pity the nation that welcomes its new ruler with trumpetings, and farewells him with hootings, only to

The Ottoman sultan on his throne, from The Better Sentences and Most Precious Dictions *by Al-Moubacchir, on vellum, 13th century.*

welcome another with trumpetings again.

"Pity the nation whose sages are dumb with years and whose strong men are yet in the cradle.

"Pity the nation divided into fragments, each fragment deeming itself a nation."

And one said: "Speak to us of that which is moving in your own heart even now."

And he looked upon that one, and there was in his voice a sound like a star singing, and he said: "In your waking dream, when you are hushed and listening to your deeper self, your thoughts, like snow-flakes, fall and flutter and garment all the sounds of your spaces with white silence.

"And what are waking dreams but clouds that bud and blossom on the sky-tree of your heart? And what are your thoughts but the petals which the winds of your heart scatter upon the hills and its fields?

"And even as you wait for peace until the formless within you takes form, so shall the cloud gather and drift until the Blessed Fingers shape its grey desire to little crystal suns and moons and stars."

Then Sarkis, he who was the half-doubter, spoke and said: "But spring shall come, and all the snows of our dreams and our thoughts shall melt and be no more."

And he answered saying: "When Spring comes to seek His beloved amongst the slumbering groves and vineyards, the snows shall indeed melt and shall run in streams to seek the river in the valley, to be the cup-bearer to the myrtle-trees and laurel.

"So shall the snow of your heart melt when your Spring is come, and thus shall your secret run in streams to seek the river of life in the valley. And the river shall enfold your secret and carry it to the great sea.

"All things shall melt and turn into songs when Spring comes. Even the stars, the vast snow-flakes that fall slowly upon the larger fields, shall melt into singing streams. When the sun of His face shall arise above the wider horizon, then what frozen symmetry would not turn into liquid melody? And who among you would not be the cup-bearer to the myrtle and the laurel?

"It was but yesterday that you were moving with the moving sea, and you were shoreless and without a self. Then the wind, the breath of Life, wove you, a veil of light on her face; then her hand gathered you and gave you form, and with a head held high you sought the heights. But the sea followed after you, and her song is still with you. And though you have forgotten your parentage, she will for ever assert her motherhood, and for ever will she call you unto her.

"In your wanderings among the mountains and the desert you will always remember the depth of her cool heart. And though oftentimes you will not know for what you long, it is indeed for her vast and rhythmic peace.

"And how else can it be? In grove and in bower when the rain dances in leaves upon the hill, when snow falls, a blessing and a covenant; in the valley when you lead your flocks to the river; in your fields where brooks, like silver streams, join together the green garment; in your gardens when the early dews mirror the heavens; in your meadows when the mist of evening half veils your way; in all these the sea is with you, a witness to your heritage, and a claim upon your love.

"It is the snow-flake in you running down to the sea."

And on a morning as they walked in the Garden, there appeared before the gate a woman, and it was Karima, she whom Almustafa had loved even as a sister in his boyhood. And she stood without, asking nothing, nor knocking with her hand upon the gate, but only gazing with longing and sadness into the Garden.

And Almustafa saw the desire upon her eyelids, and with swift steps he came to the wall and the gate and opened unto her, and she came in and was made welcome.

And she spoke and said: "Wherefore have you withdrawn yourself from us altogether, that we may not live in the light of your countenance? For behold, these many years have we loved you and waited with longing for your safe return. And now the people cry for you and would have speech with you; and I am their messenger come to beseech you that you will show yourself to the people, and speak to them out of your wisdom, and comfort the broken of heart and instruct our foolishness."

And looking upon her, he said: "Call me not wise unless you call all men wise. A young fruit am I, still clinging to the branch, and it was only yesterday that I was but a blossom.

"And call none among you foolish, for in truth we are neither wise nor foolish. We are green leaves upon the tree of life, and life itself is beyond wisdom, and surely beyond foolishness.

"And have I indeed withdrawn myself from you? Know you not that there is no distance save that which the soul does not span in fancy? And when the soul shall span that distance, it becomes a rhythm in the soul.

"The space that lies between you and your near neighbour unbefriended is indeed greater than that which lies between you and your beloved who dwells beyond seven lands and seven seas.

"For in remembrance there are no distances; and only in oblivion is there a gulf that neither your voice nor your eye can abridge.

"Between the shores of the oceans and the summit of the highest mountain there is a secret road which you must needs travel ere you become one with the sons of earth.

"And between your knowledge and your understanding there is a secret path which you must needs discover ere you become one with man, and therefore one with yourself.

"Between your right hand that gives and your left hand that receives there is a great space. Only by deeming them both giving and receiving can you bring them into spacelessness, for it is only in knowing that you have naught to give and naught to receive that you can overcome space.

"Verily the vastest distance is that which lies between your sleep-vision and your wakefulness; and between

that which is but a deed and that which is a desire.

"And there is still another road which you must needs travel ere you become one with Life. But of that road I shall not speak now, seeing that you are weary already of travelling."

Then he went forth with the woman, he and the nine, even unto the market-place, and he spoke to the people, his friends and his neighbours, and there was joy in their hearts and upon their eyelids.

And he said: "You grow in sleep, and live your fuller life in your dreaming. For all your days are spent in thanksgiving for that which you have received in the stillness of the night.

"Oftentimes you think and speak of night as the season of rest, yet in truth night is the season of seeking and finding.

"The day gives unto you the power of knowledge and

A sense of order is symbolized in the geometric tile patterns within the 17th-century Mughal mosque at Tatta, built for Shah Jahan.

teaches your fingers to become versed in the art of receiving; but it is night that leads you to the treasure-house of Life.

"The sun teaches to all things that grow their longing for the light. But it is night that raises them to the stars.

"It is indeed the stillness of the night that weaves a wedding-veil over the trees in the forest, and the flowers in the garden, and then spreads the lavish feast and makes ready the nuptial chamber; and in that holy silence tomorrow is conceived in the womb of Time.

'Thus it is with you, and thus, in seeking, you find meat and fulfilment. And though at dawn your awakening erases the memory, the board of dreams is for ever spread, and the nuptial chamber waiting."

And he was silent for a space, and they also, awaiting his word. Then he spoke again, saying: "You are spirits though you move in bodies; and, like oil that burns in the dark, you are flames though held in lamps.

"If you were naught save bodies, then my standing before you and speaking unto you would be but emptiness, even as the dead calling unto the dead. But this is not so. All that is deathless in you is free unto the day and the night and cannot be housed nor fettered, for this is the will of the Most High. You are His breath even as the wind that shall be neither caught nor caged. And I also am the breath of His breath."

And he went from their midst walking swiftly and entered again into the Garden.

And Sarkis, he who was the half-doubter, spoke and said: "And what of ugliness, Master? You speak never of ugliness."

And Almustafa answered him, and there was a whip in his

words, and he said: "My friend, what man shall call you inhospitable if he shall pass by your house, yet would not knock at your door?

"And who shall deem you deaf and unmindful if he shall speak to you in a strange tongue of which you understand nothing?

"Is it not that which you have never striven to reach, into whose heart you have never desired to enter, that you deem ugliness?

"If ugliness is aught, indeed, it is but the scales upon our eyes, and the wax filling our ears.

"Call nothing ugly, my friend, save the fear of a soul in the presence of its own memories."

And upon a day as they sat in the long shadows of the white poplars, one spoke saying: "Master, I am afraid of time. It passes over us and robs us of our youth, and what does it give in return?"

And he answered and said: "Take up now a handful of good earth. Do you find in it a seed, and perhaps a worm? If your hand were spacious and enduring enough, the seed might become a forest, and the worm a flock of angels. And forget not that the years which turn seeds to forests, and worms to angels, belong to this *Now*, all of the years, this very *Now*.

"And what are the seasons of the years save your own thoughts changing? Spring is an awakening in your breast, and summer but a recognition of your own fruitfulness. Is not autumn the ancient in you singing a lullaby to that which is still a child in your being? And what, I ask you, is winter save sleep big with the dreams of all the other seasons."

And then Mannus, the inquisitive disciple, looked about him

and he saw plants in flower cleaving unto the sycamore-tree. And he said: "Behold the parasites, Master. What say you of them? They are thieves with weary eyelids who steal the light from the streadfast children of the sun, and make fair of the sap that runneth into their branches and their leaves."

And he answered him saying: "My friend, we are all parasites. We who labour to turn the sod into pulsing life are not above those who receive life directly from the sod without knowing the sod.

"Shall a mother say to her child: 'I give you back to the forest, which is your greater mother, for you weary me, heart and hand'?

"Or shall the singer rebuke his own song, saying: 'Return now to the cave of echoes from whence you came, for your voice consumes my breath'?

"And shall the shepherd say to his yearling: 'I have no pasture whereunto I may lead you; therefore be cut off and become a sacrifice for this cause'?

"Nay, my friend, all these things are answered even before they are asked, and, like your dreams, are fulfilled ere you sleep.

"We live upon one another according to the law, ancient and timeless. Let us live thus in loving-kindness. We seek one another in our aloneness, and we walk the road when we have no hearth to sit beside.

"My friends and my brothers, the wider road is your fellow-man.

"These plants that live upon the tree draw milk of the earth in the sweet stillness of night, and the earth in her tranquil dreaming sucks at the breast of the sun.

"And the sun, even as you and I and all there is, sits in equal honour at the banquet of the Prince whose door is always open and whose board is always spread.

"Mannus, my friend, all there is lives always upon all there is; and all there is lives in the faith, shoreless, upon the bounty of the Most High."

And on a morning when the sky was yet pale with dawn, they walked all together in the Garden and looked unto the East and were silent in the presence of the rising sun.

And after a while Almustafa pointed with his hand, and he said: "The image of the morning sun in a dewdrop is not less than the sun. The reflection of life in your soul is not less than life.

"The dewdrop mirrors the light because it is one with light, and you reflect life because you and life are one.

"When darkness is upon you, say: 'This darkness is dawn not yet born; and though night's travail be full upon me, yet shall dawn be born unto me even as unto the hills.'

"The dewdrop rounding its sphere in the dusk of the lily is not unlike yourself gathering your soul in the heart of God.

"Shall a dewdrop say: 'But once in a thousand years I am even a dewdrop,' speak you and answer it saying: 'Know you not that the light of all the years is shining in your circle?'"

And on an evening a great storm visited the place, and Almustafa and his disciples, the nine, went within and sat about the fire and were silent.

Then one of the disciples said: "I am alone, Master, and the hoofs of the hours beat heavily upon my breast."

And Almustafa rose up and stood in their midst, and he said in a voice like unto the sound of a great wind: "Alone! And what of it? You came alone, and alone shall you pass into the mist.

"Therefore drink your cup alone and in silence. The autumn days have given other lips other cups and filled them with wine bitter and sweet, even as they have filled your cup.

"Drink your cup alone though it taste of your own blood and tears, and praise life for the gift of thirst. For without thirst your heart is but the shore of a barren sea, songless and without a tide.

"Drink your cup alone, and drink it with cheers.

"Raise it high above your head and drink deep to those who drink alone.

"Once I sought the company of men and sat with them at their banquet-tables and drank deep with them; but their wine did not rise to my head; nor did it flow into my bosom. It only descended to my feet. My wisdom was left dry and my heart was locked and sealed. Only my feet were with them in their fog.

"And I sought the company of men no more, nor drank wine with them at their board.

"Therefore I say unto you, though the hoofs of the hours beat heavily upon your bosom, what of it? It is well for you to drink your cup of sorrow alone, and your cup of joy shall you drink alone also."

And on a day, as Phardrous, the Greek, walked in the Garden, he struck his foot upon a stone and he was angered. And he turned and picked up the stone, saying in a low voice: "O dead thing in my path!" and he flung away the stone.

And Almustafa, the chosen and the beloved, said: "Why say you: 'O dead thing'? Have you been thus long in this Garden and know not that there is nothing dead here? All things live and glow in the knowledge of the day and the majesty of the night. You and the stone are one. There is a difference only in heart-beats. Your heart beats a little faster, does it, my friend? Ay, but it is not so tranquil.

"Its rhythm may be another rhythm, but I say unto you that if you sound the depths of your soul and scale the heights of space, you shall hear one melody, and in that melody the stone and the star sing, the one with the other, in perfect unison.

"If my words reach not your understanding, then let be until another dawn. If you have cursed this stone because in your blindness you have stumbled upon it, then would you curse a star if so be your head should encounter it in the sky. But the day will come when you will gather stones and stars as a child plucks the valley-lilies, and then shall you know that all these things are living and fragrant."

And on the first day of the week when the sounds of the temple bells sought their ears, one spoke and said: "Master, we hear much talk of God hereabout. What say you of God, and who is He in very truth?"

And he stood before them like a young tree, fearless of wind or tempest, and he answered saying: "Think now, my comrades and beloved, of a heart that contains all your hearts, a love that encompasses all your loves, a spirit that envelops all your spirits, a voice enfolding all your voices, and a silence deeper than all your silences, and timeless.

"Seek now to perceive in your selffulness a beauty more enchanting than all things beautiful, a song more vast than the songs of the sea and the forest, a majesty seated upon a throne for which Orion is but a footstool, holding a sceptre in which the Pleiades are naught save the glimmer of dewdrops.

"You have sought always only food and shelter, a garment and a staff; seek now One who is neither an aim for your arrows nor a stony cave to shield you from the elements.

"And if my words are a rock and a riddle, then seek, none the less, that your hearts may be broken, and that your questionings may bring you unto the love and the wisdom of the Most High, whom men call God."

And they were silent, every one, and they were perplexed in their heart; and Almustafa was moved with compassion for them, and he gazed with tenderness upon them and said: "Let us speak no more now of God the Father. Let us speak rather of the gods, your neighbours, and of your brothers, the elements that move about your houses and your fields.

"You would rise up in fancy unto the cloud, and you deem it height; and you would pass over the vast sea and claim it to be distance. But I say unto you that when you sow a seed in the earth, you reach a greater height; and when you hail the beauty of the morning to your neighbour, you cross a greater sea.

"Too often do you sing God, the Infinite, and yet in truth you hear not the song. Would that you might listen to the song-birds, and to the leaves that forsake the branch when the wind passes by, and forget not, my friends, that these sing only when they are separated from the branch!

"Again I bid you to speak not so freely of God, who is your All, but speak rather and understand one another, neighbour unto neighbour, a god unto a god.

"For what shall feed the fledgling in the nest if the mother bird flies skyward? And what anemone in the field shall be fulfilled unless it be husbanded by a bee from another anemone?

"It is only when you are lost in your smaller selves that you seek the sky which you call God. Would that you might find paths into your vast selves; would that you might be less idle and pave the roads!

"My mariners and my friends, it were wiser to speak less of God, whom we cannot understand, and more of each other, whom we may understand. Yet I would have you know that

we are the breath and the fragrance of God. We are God, in leaf, in flower, and oftentimes in fruit."

And on a morning when the sun was high, one of the disciples, one of those three who had played with him in childhood, approached him saying: "Master, my garment is worn, and I have no other. Give me leave to go unto the market-place and bargain that perchance I may procure me new raiment."

And Almustafa looked upon the young man, and he said: "Give me your garment." And he did so and stood naked in the noonday.

And Almustafa said in a voice that was like a young steed running upon a road: "Only the naked live in the sun. Only the artless ride the wind. And he alone who loses his way a thousand times shall have a home-coming.

"The angels are tired of the clever. And it was but yesterday that an angel said to me: 'We created hell for those who glitter. What else but fire can erase a shining surface and melt a thing to its core?'

"And I said: 'But in creating hell you created devils to govern hell.' But the angel answered: 'Nay, hell is governed by those who do not yield to fire.'

"Wise angel! He knows the ways of men and the ways of half-men. He is one of the seraphim who come to minister unto the prophets when they are tempted by the clever. And no doubt he smiles when the prophets smile, and weeps also when they weep.

"My friends and my mariners, only the naked live in the sun. Only the rudderless can sail the greater sea. Only he who is dark with the night shall wake with the dawn, and only he

who sleeps with the roots under the snow shall reach
the spring.

"For you are even like roots, and like roots are you simple,
yet you have wisdom from the earth. And you are silent,
yet you have within your unborn branches the choir of
the four winds.

"You are frail and you are formless, yet you are the
beginning of giant oaks, and of the half-pencilled pattern of
the willows against the sky.

"Once more I say, you are but roots betwixt the dark sod
and the moving heavens. And oftentimes have I seen you
rising to dance with the light, but I have also seen you shy. All
roots are shy. They have hidden their hearts so long that they
know not what to do with their hearts.

"But May shall come, and May is a restless virgin, and she
shall mother the hills and plains."

And one who had served in the Temple besought him
saying: "Teach us, Master, that our words may be even
as your words, a chant and an incense unto the people."

And Almustafa answered and said: "You shall rise beyond
your words, but your path shall remain, a rhythm and a
fragrance; a rhythm for lovers and for all who are beloved,
and a fragrance for those who would live life in a garden.

"But you shall rise beyond your words to a summit whereon
the star-dust falls, and you shall open your hands until they
are filled; then you shall lie down and sleep like a white
fledgling in a white nest, and you shall dream of your
tomorrow as white violets dream of spring.

"Ay, and you shall go down deeper than your words. You
shall seek the lost fountain-heads of the streams, and you

shall be a hidden cave echoing the faint voices of the depths which now you do not even hear.

"You shall go down deeper than your words, ay, deeper than all sounds, to the very heart of the earth, and there you shall be alone with Him who walks also upon the Milky Way."

And after a space one of the disciples asked him saying: "Master, speak to us of *being*. What is it to *be*?"

And Almustafa looked long upon him and loved him. And he stood up and walked a distance away from them; then returning, he said: "In this Garden my father and my mother lie, buried by the hands of the living; and in this Garden lie buried the seeds of yesteryear, bought hither upon the wings of the wind. A thousand times shall my mother and my father be buried here, and a thousand times shall the wind bury the seed; and a thousand years hence shall you and I and these flowers come together in this Garden even as now, and we shall *be*, loving life, and we shall *be*, dreaming of space, and we shall *be*, rising toward the sun.

"But now today to *be* is to be wise, though not a stranger to the foolish; it is to be strong, but not to the undoing of the weak; to play with young children, not as fathers, but rather as playmates who would learn their games;

"To be simple and guileless with old men and women, and to sit with them in the shade of the ancient oak-trees, though you are still walking with Spring;

"To seek a poet though he may live beyond the seven rivers, and to be at peace in his presence, nothing wanting, nothing doubting, and with no question upon your lips;

"To know that the saint and the sinner are twin brothers, whose father is our Gracious King, and that one was born but the moment before the other, wherefore we regard him as the Crowned Prince;

"To follow Beauty even when she shall lead you to the verge of the precipice; and though she is wingèd and you are wingless, and though she shall pass beyond the verge, follow her, for where Beauty is not, there is nothing;

"To be a garden without walls, a vineyard without a guardian, a treasure-house for ever open to passers-by;

"To be robbed, cheated, deceived, ay, misled and trapped and then mocked, yet with it all to look down from the height of your larger self and smile, knowing that there is a spring that will come to your garden to dance in your leaves, and an autumn to ripen your grapes; knowing that if but one of your windows is open to the East, you shall never be empty; knowing that all those deemed wrongdoers and robbers, cheaters and deceivers are your brothers in need, and that you are perchance all of these in the eyes of the blessed inhabitants of that City Invisible, above this city.

"And now, to you also whose hands fashion and find all things that are needful for the comfort of our days and our nights –

"To *be* is to be a weaver with seeing fingers, a builder mindful of light and space; to be a ploughman and feel that you are hiding a treasure with every seed you sow; to be a fisherman and a hunter with a pity for the fish and for the beast, yet a still greater pity for the hunger and need of man.

"And, above all, I say this: I would have you each and every one partners to the purpose of every man, for only so shall you hope to obtain your own good purpose.

"My comrades and my beloved, be bold and not meek; be spacious and not confined; and until my final hour and yours be indeed your greater self."

And he ceased from speaking and there fell a deep gloom upon the nine, and their heart was turned away from him, for they understood not his words.

And behold, the three men who were mariners longed for the sea; and they who had served in the Temple yearned for the consolation of her santuary; and they who had been his playfellows desired the market-place. They all were deaf to his words, so that the sound of them returned unto him like weary and homeless birds seeking refuge.

And Almustafa walked a distance from them in the Garden, saying nothing, nor looking upon them.

And they began to reason among themselves and to seek excuse for their longing to be gone.

And behold, they turned and went every man to his own place, so that Almustafa, the chosen and the beloved, was left alone.

And when the night was fully come, he took his steps to the grave-side of his mother and sat beneath the cedar-tree which grew above the place. And there came the shadow of a great light upon the sky, and the Garden shone like a fair jewel upon the breast of earth.

And Almustafa cried out in the aloneness of his spirit, and he said:

"Heavy-laden is my soul with her own ripe fruit. Who is there would come and take and be satisfied? Is there not one who has fasted and who is kindly and generous in heart, to come and break his fast upon my first yieldings to the sun and thus ease me of the weight of mine own abundance?

"My soul is running over with the wine of the ages. Is there no thirsty one to come and drink?

"Behold, there was a man standing at the cross-roads with hands stretched forth unto the passers-by, and his hands were filled with jewels. And he called upon the passers-by, saying: 'Pity me, and take from me. In God's name, take out of my hands and console me.'

"But the passers-by only looked upon him, and none took out of his hand.

"Would rather that he were a beggar stretching forth his hand to receive – ay, a shivering hand, and brought back empty to his bosom – than to stretch it forth full of rich gifts and find none to receive.

"And behold, there was also the gracious prince who raised up his silken tents between the mountain and the desert and bade his servants to burn fire, a sign to the stranger and the wanderer; and who sent forth his slaves to watch the road that they might fetch a guest. But the roads and the paths of the desert were unyielding, and they found no one.

"Would rather that prince were a man of nowhere and nowhen, seeking food and shelter. Would that he were the wanderer with naught but his staff and an earthen vessel. For then at nightfall would he meet with his kind, and with the poets of nowhere and nowhen, and share their beggary and their remembrances and their dreaming.

"And behold, the daughter of the great king rose from sleep and put upon her her silken raiment and her pearls and rubies, and she scattered musk upon her hair and dipped her fingers in amber. Then she descended from her tower to her garden, where the dew of night found her golden sandals.

"In the stillness of the night the daughter of a great king sought love in the garden, but in all the vast kingdom of her father there was none who was her lover.

"Would rather that she were the daughter of a ploughman, tending his sheep in a field, and returning to her father's house at eventide with the dust of the curving roads upon her feet, and the fragrance of the vineyards in the folds of her garment. And when the night is come, and the angel of the night is upon the world, she would steal her steps to the river-valley where her lover waits.

A Sufi shaykh greets a prince travelling along a path, in a scene from Majalis Al'Ushshaq (Assemblies of the Lovers), *Shiraz, 1550s.*

"Would that she were a nun in a cloister burning her
heart for incense, that her heart may rise to the wind, and
exhausting her spirit, a candle, for a light arising toward the
greater light, together with all those who worship and those
who love and are beloved.

"Would rather that she were a woman ancient of years,
sitting in the sun and remembering who had shared
her youth."

And the night waxed deep, and Almustafa was dark with
the night, and his spirit was as a cloud unspent. And he
cried again:

"Heavy-laden is my soul with her own ripe fruit;
Heavy-laden is my soul with her fruit.
Who now will come and eat and be fulfilled?
My soul is overflowing with her wine.
Who now will pour and drink and be cooled of the
desert heat?

"Would that I were a tree flowerless and fruitless,
For the pain of abundance is more bitter than barrenness,
And the sorrow of the rich from whom no one will take
Is greater than the grief of the beggar to whom none
would give.

"Would that I were a well, dry and parched, and men
    throwing stones into me;
For this were better and easier to be borne than to be a
    source of living water

When men pass by and will not drink.

"Would that I were a reed trodden under foot,
For that were better than to be a lyre of silvery strings
In a house whose lord has no fingers
And whose children are deaf."

Now, for seven days and seven nights no man came nigh the Garden, and he was alone with his memories and his pain; for even those who had heard his words with love and patience had turned away to the pursuits of other days.

Only Karima came, with silence upon her face like a veil; and with cup and plate within her hand, drink and meat for his aloneness and his hunger. And after setting these before him, she walked her way.

And Almustafa came again to the company of the white poplars within the gate, and he sat looking upon the road. And after a while he beheld as it were a cloud of dust blown above the road and coming toward him. And from out the cloud came the nine, and before them Karima guiding them.

And Almustafa advanced and met them upon the road, and they passed through the gate, and all was well, as though they had gone their path but an hour ago.

They came in and supped with him at his frugal board, after that Karima had laid upon it the bread and the fish and poured the last of the wine into the cups. And as she poured, she besought the Master saying: "Give me leave that I go into the city and fetch wine to replenish your cups, for this is spent."

And he looked upon her, and in his eyes were a journey and a far country, and he said: "Nay, for it is sufficent unto the hour."

And they ate and drank and were satisfied. And when it was finished, Almustafa spoke in a vast voice, deep as the sea and full as a great tide under the moon, and he said: "My comrades and my road-fellows, we must needs part this day. Long have we sailed the perilous seas, and we have climbed the steepest mountains and we have wrestled with the storms. We have known hunger, but we have also sat at wedding-feasts. Oftentimes have we been naked, but we have also worn kingly raiment. We have indeed travelled far, but now we part. Together you shall go your way, and alone must I go mine.

"And though the seas and the vast lands shall separate us, still we shall be companions upon our journey to the Holy Mountain.

"But before we go our severed roads, I would give unto you the harvest and the gleaning of my heart:

"Go you upon your way with singing, but let each song be brief, for only the songs that die young upon your lips shall live in human hearts.

"Tell a lovely truth in little words, but never an ugly truth in any words. Tell the maiden whose hair shines in the sun that

she is the daughter of the morning. But if you shall behold
the sightless, say not to him that he is one with night.

"Listen to the flute-player as it were listening to April, but if
you shall hear the critic and the fault-finder speak, be deaf as
your own bones and as distant as your fancy.

"My comrades and my beloved, upon your way you shall
meet men with hoofs; give them of your wings. And men with
horns; give them wreaths of laurel. And men with claws; give
them petals for fingers. And men with forked tongues; give
them honey for words.

"Ay, you shall meet all these and more; you shall meet the
lame selling crutches; and the blind, mirrors. And you shall
meet the rich men begging at the gate of the Temple.

"To the lame give of your swiftness, to the blind of your
vision; and see that you give of yourself to the rich beggars;
they are the most needy of all, for surely no man
would stretch a hand for alms unless he be poor indeed,
though of great possessions.

"My comrades and my friends, I charge you by our love that

A paradisial scene from One Thousand and One Nights, *contemporary
oil on canvas by Al-Attar Suad.*

you be countless paths which cross one another in the desert, where the lions and the rabbits walk, and also the wolves and the sheep.

"And remember this of me: I teach you not giving, but receiving; not denial, but fulfilment; and not yielding, but understanding, with the smile upon the lips.

"I teach you not silence, but rather a song not over-loud.

"I teach you your larger self, which contains all men."

And he rose from the board and went out straightway into the Garden and walked under the shadow of the cypress-trees as the day waned. And they followed him, at a little distance, for their heart was heavy, and their tongue clave to the roof of their mouth.

Only Karima, after she had put by the fragments, came unto him and said: "Master, I would that you suffer me to prepare food against the morrow and your journey."

And he looked upon her with eyes that saw other worlds than this, and he said: "My sister, and my beloved, it is done, even from the beginning of time. The food and the drink is ready, for the morrow, even as for our yesterday and our today.

"I go, but if I go with a truth not yet voiced, that very truth will again seek me and gather me, though my elements be scattered throughout the silences of eternity, and again shall I come before you that I may speak with a voice born anew out of the heart of those boundless silences.

"And if there be aught of beauty that I have declared not unto you, then once again shall I be called, ay, even by mine own name, Almustafa, and I shall give you a sign, that you may know I have come back to speak all that is lacking, for God will not suffer Himself to be hidden from man, nor His word to lie covered in the abyss of the heart of man.

"I shall live beyond death, and I shall sing in your ears
Even after the vast sea-wave carries me back
To the vast sea-depth.
I shall sit at your board though without a body,
And I shall go with you to your fields, a spirit invisible.
I shall come to you at your fireside, a guest unseen.
Death changes nothing but the masks that cover our faces.
The woodsman shall be still a woodsman,
The ploughman, a ploughman,
And he who sang his song to the wind shall sing it also to
   the moving spheres."

And the disciples were as still as stones, and grieved in their
heart for that he had said: "I go." But no man put out his hand
to stay the Master, nor did any follow after his footsteps.

And Almustafa went out from the Garden of his mother,
and his feet were swift and they were soundless; and in a
moment, like a blown leaf in a strong wind, he was far gone
from them, and they saw, as it were, a pale light moving up to
the heights.

And the nine walked their ways down the road. But the
woman still stood in the gathering night, and she beheld
how the light and the twilight were become one; and she
comforted her desolation and her aloneness with his words:
"I go, but if I go with a truth not yet voiced, that very truth
will seek me and gather me, and again shall I come."

And now it was eventide.
   And he had reached the hills. His steps had led him
to the mist, and he stood among the rocks and the white
cypress-trees hidden from all things, and he spoke and said:

"O Mist, my sister, white breath not yet held in a mould,
I return to you, a breath white and voiceless,
A word not yet uttered.

"O Mist, my wingèd sister mist, we are together now,
And together we shall be till life's second day,
Whose dawn shall lay you, dewdrops in a garden,
And me a babe upon the breast of a woman,
And we shall remember.

"O Mist, my sister, I come back, a heart listening in its
   depths,
Even as your heart,
A desire throbbing and aimless even as your desire,
A thought not yet gathered, even as your thought.

"O Mist, my sister, first-born of my mother,
My hands still hold the green seeds you bade me scatter,
And my lips are sealed upon the song you bade me sing;
And I bring you no fruit, and I bring you no echoes
For my hands were blind, and my lips unyielding.

"O Mist, my sister, much did I love the world, and the world
   loved me,
For all my smiles were upon her lips, and all her tears were
   in my eyes.
Yet there was between us a gulf of silence which she would
   not abridge
And I could not overstep.
"O Mist, my sister, my deathless sister Mist,
I sang the ancient songs unto my little children,

And they listened, and there was wondering upon their face;
But tomorrow perchance they will forget the song,
And I know not to whom the wind will carry the song.
And though it was not mine own, yet it came to my heart
And dwelt for a moment upon my lips.

"O Mist, my sister, though all this came to pass,
I am at peace.
It was enough to sing to those already born.
And though the singing is indeed not mine,
Yet it is of my heart's deepest desire.

"O Mist, my sister, my sister Mist,
I am one with you now.
No longer am I a self.
The walls have fallen,
And the chains have broken;
I rise to you, a mist,
And together we shall float upon the sea until life's
second day,
When dawn shall lay you, dewdrops in a garden,
And me a babe upon the breast of a woman."

PART THREE

Further Selected Writings

Contents

The Madman

God 192

The Seven Selves 196

The Three Ants 200

Night and the Madman 202

The Greater Sea 206

The Astronomer 210

Said a Blade of Grass 212

And When my Joy was Born 214

The Perfect World 216

The Forerunner

The Forerunner 220

Love 224

The King-Hermit 226

Out of My Deeper Heart 230

Beyond My Solitude 232

The Last Watch 234

Sand and Foam

Seven Times Have I Despised My Soul 240

Love and Friendship 246

Expressions of Nobility 252

The Wanderer

The Old, Old Wine 258

She Who Was Deaf 260

The River 264

God

In the ancient days, when the first quiver of speech came to my lips, I ascended the holy mountain and spoke unto God, saying, "Master, I am thy slave. Thy hidden will is my law and I shall obey thee for ever more."

But God made no answer, and like a mighty tempest passed away.

And after a thousand years I ascended the holy mountain and again spoke unto God, saying, "Creator, I am thy creation. Out of clay hast thou fashioned me and to thee I owe mine all."

And God made no answer, but like a thousand swift wings passed away.

And after a thousand years I climbed the holy mountain and spoke unto God again, saying, "Father, I am thy son. In pity and love thou hast given me birth, and through love and worship I shall inherit thy kingdom."

And God made no answer, and like the mist that veils the distant hills he passed away.

And after a thousand years I climbed the sacred mountain and again spoke unto God, saying, "My God, my aim and my fulfilment; I am thy yesterday and thou are my tomorrow. I am thy root in the earth and thou art my flower in the sky, and together we grow before the face of the sun."

Then God leaned over me, and in my ears whispered words of sweetness, and even as the sea that enfoldeth a brook that runneth down to her, he enfolded me.

And when I descended to the valleys and the plains God was there also.

*Paradise is represented in this detail from a 17th-century Mughal carpet
made out of silk interwoven with silver thread.*

The Seven Selves

In the stillest hour of the night, as I lay half asleep, my seven selves sat together and thus conversed in whispers:

First Self: Here, in this madman, I have dwelt all these years, with naught to do but renew his pain by day and recreate his sorrow by night. I can bear my fate no longer, and now I rebel.

Second Self: Yours is a better lot than mine, brother, for it is given to me to be this madman's joyous self. I laugh his laughter and sing his happy hours, and with thrice winged feet I dance his brighter thoughts. It is I that would rebel against my weary existence.

Third Self: And what of me, the love-ridden self, the flaming brand of wild passion and fantastic desires? It is I the love-sick self who would rebel against this madman.

Fourth Self: I, amongst you all, am the most miserable, for naught was given me but odious hatred and destructive loathing. It is I, the tempest-like self, the one born in the black caves of Hell, who would protest against serving this madman.

A 17th-century Ottoman hanging made out of linen delicately embroidered with silk thread.

Fifth Self: Nay, it is I, the thinking self, the fanciful self, the self of hunger and thirst, the one doomed to wander without rest in search of unknown things and things not yet created; it is I, not you, who would rebel.

Sixth Self: And I, the working self, the pitiful labourer, who, with patient hands, and longing eyes, fashion the days into images and give the formless elements new and eternal forms – it is I, the solitary one, who would rebel against this restless madman.

Seventh Self: How strange that you all would rebel against this man, because each and every one of you has a

preordained fate to fulfill. Ah! could I but be like one of you,
a self with a determined lot! But I have none, I am the
do-nothing self, the one who sits in the dumb, empty
nowhere and nowhen, while you are busy re-creating life.
Is it you or I, neighbours, who should rebel?

When the seventh self thus spake the other six selves looked
with pity upon him but said nothing more; and as the night
grew deeper one after the other went to sleep enfolded with a
new and happy submission.

But the seventh self remained watching and gazing at
nothingness, which is behind all things.

The Three Ants

Three ants met on the nose of a man who was asleep in the sun. And after they had saluted one another, each according to the custom of his tribe, they stood there conversing.

The first ant said, "These hills and plains are the most barren I have known. I have searched all day for a grain of some sort, and there is none to be found."

Said the second ant, "I too have found nothing, though I have visited every nook and glade. This is, I believe, what my people call the soft, moving land where nothing grows."

Then the third ant raised his head and said, "My friends, we are standing now on the nose of the Supreme Ant, the mighty and infinite Ant, whose body is so great that we cannot see it, whose shadow is so vast that we cannot trace it, whose voice is so loud that we cannot hear it; and He is omnipresent."

When the third ant spoke thus the other ants looked at each other and laughed.

At that moment the man moved and in his sleep raised his hand and scratched his nose, and the three ants were crushed.

Like trails of insects, the brickwork patterns of the vaulted ceiling of a building in Shiraz, Iran, radiate towards the centre.

Night and the Madman

"I am like thee, O, Night, dark and naked; I walk on
the flaming path which is above my day-dreams, and
whenever my foot touches earth a giant oak tree comes forth."

"Nay, thou art not like me, O, Madman, for thou still
lookest backward to see how large a foot-print thou leavest
on the sand."

"I am like thee, O, Night, silent and deep; and in the heart of
my loneliness lies a Goddess in child-bed; and in him who is
being born Heaven touches Hell."

"Nay, thou art not like me, O, Madman, for thou shudderest
yet before pain, and the song of the abyss terrifies thee."

"I am like thee, O, Night, wild and terrible; for my ears are
crowded with cries of conquered nations and sighs for
forgotten lands."

"Nay, thou art not like me, O, Madman, for thou still takest
thy little-self for a comrade, and with thy monster-self thou
canst not be friend."

"I am like thee, O, Night, cruel and awful; for my bosom is lit by burning ships at sea, and my lips are wet with blood of slain warriors."

"Nay, thou art not like me, O, Madman; for the desire for a sister-spirit is yet upon thee, and thou hast not become a law unto thyself."

"I am like thee, O, Night, joyous and glad; for he who dwells in my shadow is now drunk with virgin wine, and she who follows me is sinning mirthfully."

"Nay, thou art not like me, O, Madman, for thy soul is wrapped in the veil of seven folds and thou holdest not thy heart in thine hand."

"I am like thee, O, Night, patient and passionate; for in my breast a thousand dead lovers are buried in shrouds of withered kisses."

"Yea, Madman, art thou like me? Art thou like me?
And canst thou ride the tempest as a steed, and grasp
the lightning as a sword?"

"Like thee, O, Night, like thee, mighty and high, and my
throne is built upon heaps of fallen Gods; and before me too
pass the days to kiss the hem of my garment but never to gaze
at my face."

"Art thou like me, child of my darkest heart? And dost thou
think my untamed thoughts and speak my vast language?"

"Yea, we are twin brothers, O, Night; for thou revealest space
and I reveal my soul."

The Greater Sea

My soul and I went to the great sea to bathe. And when we reached the shore, we went about looking for a hidden and lonely place.

But as we walked, we saw a man sitting on a grey rock taking pinches of salt from a bag and throwing them into the sea.

"This is the pessimist," said my soul, "Let us leave this place. We cannot bathe here."

We walked on until we reached an inlet. There we saw, standing on a white rock, a man holding a bejewelled box, from which he took sugar and threw it into the sea.

"And this is the optimist," said my soul, "And he too must not see our naked bodies."

Further on we walked. And on a beach we saw a man picking up dead fish and tenderly putting them back into the water.

"And we cannot bathe before him," said my soul. "He is the humane philanthropist."

And we passed on.

Then we came where we saw a man tracing his shadow on the sand. Great waves came and erased it. But he went on tracing it again and again.

"He is the mystic," said my soul, "Let us leave him."

And we walked on, till in a quiet cover we saw a man scooping up the foam and putting it into an alabaster bowl.

"He is the idealist," said my soul, "Surely he must not see our nudity."

And on we walked. Suddenly we heard a voice crying, "This is the sea. This is the deep sea. This is the vast and mighty sea." And when we reached the voice it was a man whose back was turned to the sea, and at his ear he held a shell, listening to its murmur.

And my soul said, "Let us pass on. He is the realist, who turns his back on the whole he cannot grasp, and busies himself with a fragment."

So we passed on. And in a weedy place among the rocks was a man with his head buried in the sand. And I said to my soul, "We can bath here, for he cannot see us."

"Nay," said my soul, "For he is the most deadly of them all. He is the puritan."

Then a great sadness came over the face of my soul, and into her voice.

"Let us go hence," she said, "For there is no lonely, hidden place where we can bathe. I would not have this wind lift my golden hair, or bare my white bosom in this air, or let the light disclose my sacred nakedness."

Then we left that sea to seek the Greater Sea.

The Astronomer

In the shadow of the temple my friend and I saw a blind man sitting alone. And my friend said, "Behold the wisest man of our land."

Then I left my friend and approached the blind man and greeted him. And we conversed.

After a while I said, "Forgive my question; but since when has thou been blind?"

"From my birth," he answered.

Said I, "And what path of wisdom followest thou?"

Said he, "I am an astronomer."

Then he placed his hand upon his breast saying, "I watch all these suns and moons and stars."

Said a Blade of Grass

Said a blade of grass to an autumn leaf, "You make such a noise falling! You scatter all my winter dreams."

Said the leaf indignant, "Low-born and low-dwelling! Songless, peevish thing! You live not in the upper air and you cannot tell the sound of singing."

Then the autumn leaf lay down upon the earth and slept. And when spring came she waked again – and she was a blade of grass.

And when it was autumn and her winter sleep was upon her, and above her through all the air the leaves were falling, she muttered to herself, "O these autumn leaves! They make such a noise! They scatter all my winter dreams."

Silk- and metal-thread embroidery on a silk cushion cover in a design that resembles falling foliage. Ottoman, 16th–17th century.

And When my Joy was Born

And when my Joy was born, I held it in my arms and stood on the house-top shouting, "Come ye, my neighbours, come and see, for Joy this day is born unto me. Come and behold this gladsome thing that laugheth in the sun."

But none of my neighbours came to look upon my Joy, and great was my astonishment.

And every day for seven moons I proclaimed my Joy from the house-top – and yet no one heeded me. And my Joy and I were alone, unsought and unvisited.

Then my Joy grew pale and weary because no other heart but mine held its loveliness and no other lips kissed its lips.

Then my Joy died of isolation.

And now I only remember my dead Joy in remembering my dead Sorrow. But memory is an autumn leaf that murmurs a while in the wind and then is heard no more.

A cotton-dresser from Miftah al-Fuzala, *a 15th-century glossary of rare words by Persian poet Shadiyabadi (his name means "from the city of joy").*

The Perfect World

God of lost souls, thou who are lost amongst the gods, hear me:

Gentle Destiny that watchest over us, mad, wandering spirits, hear me:

I dwell in the midst of a perfect race, I the most imperfect.

I, a human chaos, a nebula of confused elements, I move amongst finished worlds – peoples of complete laws and pure order, whose thoughts are assorted, whose dreams are arranged, and whose visions are enrolled and registered.

Their virtues, O God, are measured, their sins are weighed, and even the countless things that pass in the dim twilight of neither sin nor virtue are recorded and catalogued.

Here days and night are divided into seasons of conduct and governed by rules of blameless accuracy.

To eat, to drink, to sleep, to cover one's nudity, and then to be weary in due time.

To work, to play, to sing, to dance, and then to lie still when the clock strikes the hour.

To think thus, to feel thus much, and then to cease thinking and feeling when a certain star rises above yonder horizon.

To rob a neighbour with a smile, to bestow gifts with a graceful wave of the hand, to praise prudently, to blame cautiously, to destroy a soul with a word, to burn a body with a breath, and then to wash the hands when the day's work is done.

To love according to an established order, to entertain one's best self in a preconceived manner, to worship the gods becomingly, to intrigue the devils artfully – and then to forget all as though memory were dead.

To fancy with a motive, to contemplate with consideration, to be happy sweetly, to suffer nobly – and then to empty the cup so that tomorrow may fill it again.

All these things, O God, are conceived with forethought, born with determination, nursed with exactness, governed by rules, directed by reason, and then slain and buried after a prescribed method. And even their silent graves that lie within the human soul are marked and numbered.

It is a perfect world, a world of consummate excellence, a world of supreme wonders, the ripest fruit in God's garden, the master-thought of the universe.

But why should I be here, O God, I a green seed of unfulfilled passion, a mad tempest that seeketh neither east nor west, a bewildered fragment from a burnt planet?

Why am I here, O God of lost souls, thou who art lost amongst the gods?

The Forerunner

You are your own forerunner, and the towers you have builded are but the foundation of your giant-self. And that self too shall be a foundation.

And I too am my own forerunner, for the long shadow stretching before me at sunrise shall gather under my feet at the noon hour. Yet another sunrise shall lay another shadow before me, and that also shall be gathered at another noon.

Always have we been our own forerunners, and always shall we be. And all that we have gathered and shall gather shall be but seeds for fields yet unploughed. We are the fields and the ploughmen, the gatherers and the gathered.

When you were a wandering desire in the mist, I too was there, a wandering desire. Then we sought one another, and out of our eagerness dreams were born. And dreams were time limitless, and dreams were space without measure.

And when you were a silent word upon Life's quivering lips, I too was there, another silent word. Then Life uttered us and we came down the years throbbing with memories of yesterday and with longing for tomorrow, for yesterday was death conquered and tomorrow was birth pursued.

And now we are in God's hands. You are a sun in His right hand and I an earth in His left hand. Yet you are not more, shining, than I, shone upon.

*A green glazed bottle adorned with a scene, set in a garden, of a man
watching a dancer, 17th-century Iran.*

And we, sun and earth, are but the beginning of a greater sun and a greater earth. And always shall we be the beginning.

You are your own forerunner, you the stranger passing by the gate of my garden.
And I too am my own forerunner, though I sit in the shadows of my trees and seem motionless

Love

They say the jackal and the mole
Drink from the self-same stream
Where the lion comes to drink.

And they say the eagle and the vulture
Dig their beaks into the same carcass,
And are at peace, one with the other,
In the presence of the dead thing.

O love, whose lordly hand
Has bridled my desires,
And raised my hunger and my thirst
To dignity and pride,
Let not the strong in me and the constant
Eat the bread or drink the wine
That tempt my weaker self.
Let me rather starve,
And let my heart parch with thirst,
And let me die and perish,
Ere I stretch my hand
To a cup you did not fill,
Or a bowl you did not bless.

A Persian prince entertains a female companion in a park, depicted in a
fresco from the early 17th century in Isfahan, Iran.

The King-Hermit

They told me that in a forest among the mountains lives a young man in solitude who once was a king of a vast country beyond the Two Rivers. And they also said that he, of his own will, had left his throne and the land of his glory and come to dwell in the wilderness.

And I said, "I would seek that man, and learn the secret of his heart; for he who renounces a kingdom must needs be greater than a kingdom."

On that very day I went to the forest where he dwells. And I found him sitting under a white cypress, and in his hand a reed as if it were a sceptre. And I greeted him even as I would greet a king.

And he turned to me and said gently, "What would you in this forest of serenity? Seek you a lost self in the green shadows, or is it a home-coming in your twilight?"

And I answered, "I sought but you — for I fain would know that which made you leave a kingdom for a forest."

And he said, "Brief is my story, for sudden was the bursting of the bubble. It happened thus: One day as I sat at a window in my palace, my chamberlain and an envoy from a foreign land were walking in my garden. And as they approached my window, the lord chamberlain was speaking of himself and saying, 'I am like the king; I have a thirst for strong wine and

A man on horseback encounters a lone bather in a stream, a miniature on vellum from the epic Khamsa of the poet Nizami, 16th century, Iran.

a hunger for all games of chance. And like my lord the king I have storms of temper.' And the lord chamberlain and the envoy disappeared among the trees. But in a few minutes they returned, and this time the lord chamberlain was speaking of me, and he was saying, 'My lord the king is like myself – a good marksman; and like me he loves music and bathes thrice a day.' "

After a moment he added, "On the eve of that day I left my palace with but my garment, for I would no longer be ruler over those who assume my vices and attribute to me their virtues."

And I said, "This is indeed a wonder, and passing strange."

And he said, "Nay, my friend, you knocked at the gate of my silences and received but a trifle. For who would not leave a kingdom for a forest where the seasons sing and dance ceaselessly? Many are those who have given their kingdom for less than solitude and the sweet fellowship of aloneness. Countless are the eagles who descend from the upper air to live with moles that they may know the secrets of the earth. There are those who renounce the kingdom of dreams that they may not seem distant from the dreamless. And those who renounce the kingdom of nakedness and cover their souls that others may not be ashamed in beholding truth uncovered and beauty unveiled. And greater yet than all of these is he who renounces the kingdom of sorrow that he may not seem proud and vainglorious."

Then rising he leaned upon his reed and said, "Go now to the great city and sit at its gate and watch all those who enter into it and those who go out. And see that you find him who, though born a king, is without kingdom; and him who though ruled in flesh rules in spirit – though neither he nor his subjects know this; and him also who but seems to rule yet is in truth slave of his own slaves."

After he had said these things he smiled on me, and there were a thousand dawns upon his lips. Then he turned and walked away into the heart of the forest.

And I returned to the city, and I sat at its gate to watch the passersby even as he had told me. And from that day to this numberless are the kings whose shadows have passed over me and few are the subjects over whom my shadow passed.

Out of My Deeper Heart

Out of my deeper heart a bird rose and flew skywards. Higher and higher did it rise, yet larger and larger did it grow.

At first it was but like a swallow, then a lark, then an eagle, then as vast as a spring cloud, and then it filled the starry heavens.

Out of my heart a bird flew skyward. And it waxed larger as it flew. Yet it left not my heart.

O my faith, my untamed knowledge, how shall I fly to your height and see with you man's larger self pencilled upon the sky?

How shall I turn this sea within me into mist, and move with you in space immeasurable?

How can a prisoner within the temple behold its golden domes?

How shall the heart of a fruit be stretched to envelop the fruit also?

O my faith, I am in chains behind these bars of silver and ebony, and I cannot fly with you.

Yet out of my heart you rise skyward, and it is my heart that holds you, and I shall be content.

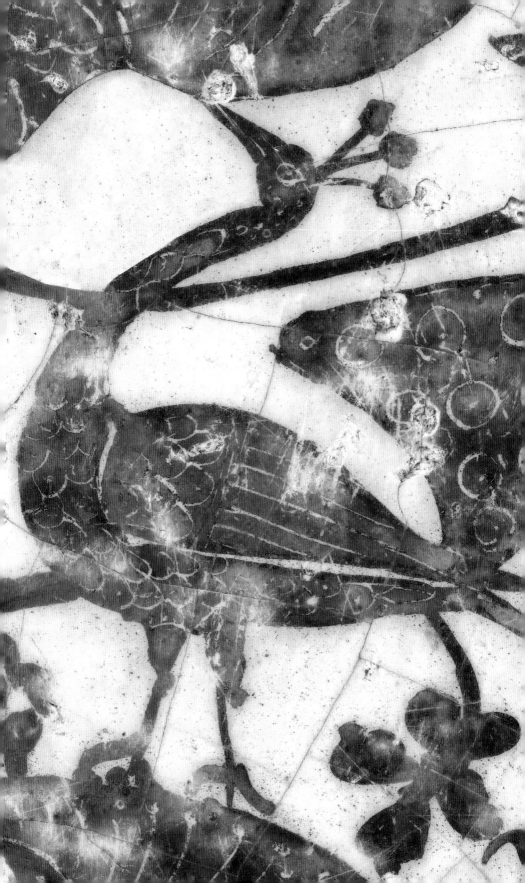

Beyond My Solitude

Beyond my solitude is another solitude, and to him who dwells therein my aloneness is a crowded market-place and my silence a confusion of sounds.

Too young am I and too restless to seek that above-solitude. The voices of yonder valley still hold my ears and its shadows bar my way and I cannot go.

Beyond these hills is a grove of enchantment and to him who dwells therein my peace is but a whirlwind and my enchantment an illusion.

Too young am I and too riotous to seek that sacred grove. The taste of blood is clinging in my mouth, and the bow and the arrows of my fathers yet linger in my hand and I cannot go.

Beyond this burdened self lives my freer self; and to him my dreams are a battle fought in twilight and my desires the rattling of bones.

Too young am I and too outraged to be my freer self.

And how shall I become my freer self unless I slay my burdened selves, or unless all men become free?

How shall the eagle in me soar against the sun until my fledglings leave the nest which I with my own beak have built for them?

A 13th-century metalwork vase from Aleppo that once belonged to Saladin, which is intricately decorated with hunters armed with bows.

The Last Watch

At the high tide of night, when the first breath of dawn came upon the wind, the Forerunner, he who calls himself echo to a voice yet unheard, left his bed-chamber and ascended to the roof of his house. Long he stood and looked down upon the slumbering city. Then he raised his head, and even as if the sleepless spirits of all those asleep had gathered around him, he opened his lips and spoke, and he said:

"My friends and neighbours and you who daily pass my gate, I would speak to you in your sleep, and in the valley of your dreams I would walk naked and unrestrained; far heedless are your waking hours and deaf are your sound-burdened ears.

"Long did I love you and overmuch.

"I love the one among you as though he were all, and all as if you were one. And in the spring of my heart I sang in your gardens, and in the summer of my heart I watched at your threshing-floors.

"Yea, I loved you all, the giant and the pygmy, the leper and the anointed, and him who gropes in the dark even as him who dances his days upon the mountains.

"You, the strong, have I loved, though the marks of your iron hoofs are yet upon my flesh; and you the weak, though you have drained my faith and wasted my patience.

"You the rich have I loved, while bitter was your honey to

A 12-pointed star wall tile pattern from the Jamia mosque, built at Tatta in Mughal India by Shah Jahan (ruled 1627–1658).

my mouth; and you the poor, though you knew my empty-handed shame.

"You the poet with the barrowed lute and blind fingers, you have I loved in self-indulgence; and you the scholar, ever gathering rotted shrouds in potters' fields.

"You the priest I have loved, who sit in the silences of yesterday questioning the fate of my tomorrow; and you the worshippers of gods the images of your own desires.

"You the thirsting woman whose cup is ever full, I have loved you in understanding; and you the woman of restless nights, you too I have loved in pity.

"You the talkative have I loved, saying, 'Life hath much to say'; and you the dumb have I loved, whispering to myself, 'Says he not in silence that which I fain would hear in words?'

"And you the judge and the critic, I have loved also; yet when you have seen me crucified, you said, 'He bleeds rhythmically, and the pattern his blood makes upon his white skin is beautiful to behold.'

"Yea, I have loved you all, the young and the old, the trembling reed and the oak.

"But alas! it was the over-abundance of my heart that turned you from me. You would drink love from a cup, but not from a surging river. You would hear love's faint murmur, but when love shouts you would muffle your ears.

"And because I have loved you all you have said, 'Too soft and yielding is his heart, and too undiscerning is his path. It is the love of a needy one, who picks crumbs even as he sits at kingly feasts. And it is the love of a weakling, for the strong loves only the strong.'

"And because I have loved you overmuch you have said, 'It is but the love of a blind man who knows not the beauty of one nor the ugliness of another. And it is the love of the tasteless who drinks vinegar even as wine. And it is the love of the impertinent and the overweening, for what stranger could be our mother and father and sister and brother?'

"This you have said, and more. For often in the marketplace you pointed your fingers at me and said mockingly, 'There goes the ageless one, the man without seasons, who at the noon hour plays games with our children and at eventide sits with our elders and assumes wisdom and understanding.'

"And I said, 'I will love them more. Aye, even more. I will hide my love with seeming to hate, and disguise my tenderness as bitterness. I will wear an iron mask, and only when armed and mailed shall I seek them.'

"Then I laid a heavy hand upon your bruises, and like a tempest in the night I thundered in your ears.

"From the housetop I proclaimed you hypocrites, pharisees, tricksters, false and empty earth-bubbles.

"The short-sighted among you I cursed for blind bats, and those too near the earth I likened to soulless moles.

"The eloquent I pronounced fork-tongued, the silent, stone-lipped, and the simple and artless I called the dead never weary of death.

"The seekers after world knowledge I condemned as offenders of the holy spirit and those who would naught but the spirit I branded as hunters of shadows who cast their nets in flat waters and catch but their own images.

"Thus with my lips have I denounced you, while my heart,

bleeding within me, called you tender names.

"It was love lashed by its own self that spoke. It was pride half slain that fluttered in the dust. It was my hunger for your love that raged from the housetop, while my own love, kneeling in silence, prayed your forgiveness.

"But behold a miracle!

"It was my disguise that opened your eyes, and my seeming to hate that woke your hearts.

"And now you love me.

"You love the swords that strike you and the arrows that crave your breast. For it comforts you to be wounded and only when you drink of your own blood can you be intoxicated.

"Like moths that seek destruction in the flame you gather daily in my garden; and with faces uplifted and eyes enchanted you watch me tear the fabric of your days. And in whispers you say the one to the other, 'He sees with the light of God. He speaks like the prophets of old.

He unveils our souls and unlocks our hearts, and like the eagle that knows the way of foxes he knows our ways.'

"Aye, in truth, I know your ways, but only as an eagle knows the ways of his fledglings. And I fain would disclose my secret. Yet in my need for your nearness I feign remoteness, and in fear of the ebb-tide of your love I guard the floodgates of my love."

After saying these things the Forerunner covered his face with his hands and wept bitterly. For he knew in his heart that love humiliated in its nakedness is greater than love that seeks triumph in disguise; and he was ashamed.

But suddenly he raised his head, and like one waking from sleep he outstretched his arms and said, "Night is over, and we children of night must die when dawn comes leaping upon the hills; and out of our ashes a mightier love shall rise. And it shall laugh in the sun, and it shall be deathless."

Seven Times Have I Despised My Soul

I am forever walking upon these shores,
Betwixt the sand and the foam,
The high tide will erase my foot-prints,
And the wind will blow away the foam.
But the sea and the shore will remain
Forever.

Once I filled my hand with mist.
Then I opened it and lo, the mist was a worm.
And I closed and opened my hand again, and behold there
was a bird.
And again I closed and opened my hand, and in its hollow
stood a man with a sad face, turned upward.
And again I closed my hand, and when I opened it there was
naught but mist.
But I heard a song of exceeding sweetness.

It was but yesterday I thought myself a fragment quivering
without rhythm in the sphere of life.
Now I know that I am the sphere, and all life in rhythmic
fragments moves within me.

They say to me in their awakening, "You and the world you live in are but a grain of sand upon the infinite shore of an infinite sea."

And in my dream I say to them, "I am the infinite sea, and all worlds are but grains of sand upon my shore."

Only once have I been made mute. It was when a man asked me, "Who are you?"

The first thought of God was an angel.
The first word of God was a man.

We were fluttering, wandering, longing creatures a thousand thousand years before the sea and the wind in the forest gave us words.

Now how can we express the ancient of days in us with only the sounds of our yesterdays?

The Sphinx spoke only once, and the Sphinx said, "A grain of sand is a desert, and a desert is a grain of sand; and now let us all be silent again."

I heard the Sphinx, but I did not understand.

Long did I lie in the dust of Egypt, silent and unaware of the seasons.

Then the sun gave me birth, and I rose and walked upon the banks of the Nile,

Singing with the days and dreaming with the nights.

And now the sun treads upon me with a thousand feet that I may lie again in the dust of Egypt.

But behold a marvel and a riddle!
The very sun that gathered me cannot scatter me.
Still erect am I, and sure of foot do I walk upon the banks
of the Nile.

Remembrance is a form of meeting.

Forgetfulness is a form of freedom.

We measure time according to the movement of countless
suns; and they measure time by little machines in their
little pockets.
Now tell me, how could we ever meet at the same place and
the same time?

Space is not space between the earth and the sun to one who
looks down from the windows of the Milky Way.

Humanity is a river of light running from the ex-eternity
to eternity.

Do not the spirits who dwell in the ether envy man his pain?

On my way to the Holy City I met another pilgrim and I
asked him, "Is this indeed the way to the Holy City?"
And he said, "Follow me, and you will reach the Holy City
in a day and a night."
And I followed him. And we walked many days and many
nights, yet we did not reach the Holy City.

And what was to my surprise he became angry with me because he had misled me.

Make me, oh God, the prey of the lion, ere You make the rabbit my prey.

One may not reach the dawn save by the path of the night.

My house says to me, "Do not leave me, for here dwells your past."
And the road says to me, "Come and follow me, for I am your future."
And I say to both my house and the road, "I have no past, nor have I a future. If I stay here, there is a going in my staying; and if I go there is a staying in my going. Only love and death change all things."

How can I lose faith in the justice of life, when the dreams of those who sleep upon feathers are not more beautiful than the dreams of those who sleep upon the earth?

Strange, the desire for certain pleasures is a part of my pain.

Seven times have I despised my soul:
The first time when I saw her being meek that she might attain height.
The second time when I saw her limping before the crippled.
The third time when she was given to choose between the hard and the easy, and she chose the easy.
The fourth time when she committed a wrong, and comforted herself that others also commit wrong.
The fifth time when she forbore for weakness, and attributed her patience to strength.
The sixth time when she despised the ugliness of a face, and knew not that it was one of her own masks.
And the seventh time when she sang a song of praise, and deemed it a virtue.

Love and Friendship

A poet is a dethroned king sitting among the ashes of his palace trying to fashion an image out of the ashes.

Poetry is a deal of joy and pain and wonder, with a dash of the dictionary.

In vain shall a poet seek the mother of the songs of his heart.

Once I said to a poet, "We shall not know your worth until you die."
And he answered saying, "Yes, death is always the revealer. And if indeed you would know my worth it is that I have more in my heart than upon my tongue, and more in my desire than in my hand."

If you sing of beauty though alone in the heart of the desert you will have an audience.

Poetry is wisdom that enchants the heart.
Wisdom is poetry that sings in the mind.
If we could enchant man's heart and at the same time sing in his mind,
Then in truth he would live in the shadow of God.

Inspiration will always sing; inspiration will never explain.

We often sing lullabyes to our children that we ourselves may sleep.

All our words are but crumbs that fall down from the feast of the mind.

Thinking is always the stumbling stone to poetry.

A great singer is he who sings our silences.

How can you sing if your mouth be filled with food?
How shall your hand be raised in blessing if it is filled with gold?

They say the nightingale pierces his bosom with a thorn when he sings his love song.
So do we all. How else should we sing?

Genius is but a robin's song at the beginning of a slow spring.

Even the most winged spirit cannot escape physical necessity.

A madman is not less a musician than you or myself; only the instrument on which he plays is a little out of tune.

The song that lies silent in the heart of a mother sings upon the lips of her child.

No longing remains unfulfilled.

I have never agreed with my other self wholly. The truth of the matter seems to lie between us.

Your other self is always sorry for you. But your other self grows on sorrow; so all is well.

There is no struggle of soul and body save in the minds of those whose souls are asleep and whose bodies are out of tune.

When you reach the heart of life you shall find beauty in all things, even in the eyes that are blind to beauty.

We live only to discover beauty. All else is a form of waiting.

Sow a seed and the earth will yield you a flower. Dream your dream to the sky and it will bring you your beloved.

The devil died the very day you were born.
Now you do not have to go through hell to meet an angel.

Many a woman borrows a man's heart; very few could possess it.

If you would possess you must not claim.

When a man's hand touches the hand of a woman they both touch the heart of eternity.

Love is the veil between lover and lover.

Every man loves two women; the one is the creation of his imagination, and the other is not yet born.

Men who do not forgive women their little faults will never enjoy their great virtues.

Love that does not renew itself every day becomes a habit and in turn a slavery.

Lovers embrace that which is between them rather than each other.

Love and doubt have never been on speaking terms.

Love is a word of light, written by a hand of light, upon a page of light.
Friendship is always a sweet responsibility, never an opportunity.

If you do not understand your friend under all conditions you will never understand him.

Your most radiant garment is of the other person's weaving;
Your most savoury meal is that which you eat at the other person's table;

Your most comfortable bed is in the other person's house.
Now tell me, how can you separate yourself from the other person?

Your mind and my heart will never agree until your mind ceases to live in numbers and my heart in the mist.

We shall never understand one another until we reduce the language to seven words.

Expressions of Nobility

If it were not for our conception of weights and measures we would stand in awe of the firefly as we do before the sun.

A scientist without imagination is a butcher with dull knives and out-worn scales.
But what would you, since we are not all vegetarians?

When you sing the hungry hears you with his stomach.

Death is not nearer to the aged than to the new-born; neither is life.

If indeed you must be candid, be candid beautifully; otherwise keep silent, for there is a man in our neighbourhood who is dying.

Mayhap a funeral among men is a wedding feast among the angels.

A forgotten reality may die and leave in its will seven thousand actualities and facts to be spent in its funeral and the building of a tomb.

In truth we talk only to ourselves, but sometimes we talk loud enough that others may hear us.

The obvious is that which is never seen until someone expresses it simply.

If the Milky Way were not within me how should I have seen it or known it?

Unless I am a physician among physicians they would not believe that I am an astronomer.

Perhaps the sea's definition of a shell is the pearl. Perhaps time's definition of coal is the diamond.

Fame is the shadow of passion standing in the light.

A root is a flower that disdains fame.

There is neither religion nor science beyond beauty.

Every great man I have known had something small in his make-up; and it was that small something which prevented inactivity or madness or suicide.

The truly great man is he who would master no one, and who would be mastered by none.

I would not believe that a man is a mediocre simply because he kills the criminals and the prophets.

Tolerance is love sick with the sickness of haughtiness.

Worms will turn; but is it not strange that even elephants will yield?

A disagreement may be the shortest cut between two minds.

I am the flame and I am the dry bush, and one part of me consumes the other part.

We are all seeking the summit of the holy moutain; but shall not our road be shorter if we consider the past a chart and not a guide?

Wisdom ceases to be wisdom when it becomes too proud to weep, too grave to laugh, and too self-ful to seek other than itself.

Had I filled myself with all that you know what room should I have for all that you do not know?

I have learned silence from the talkative, toleration from the intolerant, and kindness from the unkind; yet strange, I am ungrateful to these teachers.

A bigot is a stone-deaf orator.

The silence of the envious is too noisy.

When you reach the end of what you should know, you will be at the beginning of what you should sense.

An exaggeration is a truth that has lost its temper.

If you can see only what light reveals and hear only what
sound announces,
   Then in truth you do not see nor do you hear.

A fact is a truth unsexed.

You cannot laugh and be unkind at the same time.

The nearest to my heart are a king without a kingdom and a
poor man who does not know how to beg.

A shy failure is nobler than an immodest success.

Dig anywhere in the earth and you will find a treasure, only
you must dig with the faith of a peasant.

Said a hunted fox followed by twenty horsemen and a pack
of twenty hounds, "Of course they will kill me. But how
poor and how stupid they must be. Surely it would not be
worth while for twenty foxes riding on twenty asses and
accompanied by twenty wolves to chase and kill one man."

It is the mind in us that yields to the laws made by us, but
never the spirit in us.

A traveller am I and a navigator, and every day I discover a new region within my soul.

A woman protested saying, "Of course it was a righteous war. My son fell in it."

I said to Life, "I would hear Death speak."
And Life raised her voice a little higher and said, "You hear him now."

When you have solved all the mysteries of life you long for death, for it is but another mystery of life.

Birth and death are the two noblest expressions of bravery.

My friend, you and I shall remain strangers unto life,
And unto one another, and each unto himself,
Until the day when you shall speak and I shall listen
Deeming your voice my own voice;
And when I shall stand before you
Thinking myself standing before a mirror.

They say to me, "Should you know yourself you would know all men."
And I say, "Only when I seek all men shall I know myself."

The Old, Old Wine

Once there lived a rich man who was justly proud of his cellar and the wine therein. And there was one jug of ancient vintage kept for some occasion known only to himself.

The governor of the state visited him, and he bethought him and said, "That jug shall not be opened for a mere governor."

And a bishop of the diocese visited him, but he said to himself, "Nay, I will not open that jug. He would not know its value, nor would its aroma reach his nostrils."

The prince of the realm came and supped with him. But he thought, "It is too royal a wine for a mere princeling."

And even on the day when his own nephew was married, he said to himself, "No, not to these guests shall that jug be brought forth."

And the years passed by, and he died, an old man, and he was buried like unto every seed and acorn.

And upon the day that he was buried the ancient jug was brought out together with other jugs of wine, and it was shared by the peasants of the neighborhood. And none knew its great age.

To them, all that is poured into a cup is only wine.

A mural from the Chehel Sotoun ("Forty Pillars") palace of the Safavid ruler Shah Abbas II in Isfahan, Iran, shows a man with a wine bottle.

She Who Was Deaf

Once there lived a rich man who had a young wife, and she was stone deaf.

And upon a morning when they were breaking their feast, she spoke to him and she said, "Yesterday I visited the market place, and there were exhibited silken raiment from Damascus, and coverchiefs from India, necklaces from Persia, and bracelets from Yamman. It seems that the caravans had but just brought these things to our city. And now behold me, in rags, yet the wife of a rich man. I would have some of those beautiful things."

The husband, still busy with his morning coffee said, "My dear, there is *no* reason why you should not go down to the Street and buy all that your heart may desire."

And the deaf wife said, "'No!' You always say, 'No, no.' Must I needs appear in tatters among our friends to shame your wealth and my people?"

And the husband said, "I did not say, 'No.' You may go forth freely to the market place and purchase the most beautiful apparel and jewels that have come to our city."

But again the wife mis-read his words, and she replied, "Of all rich men you are the most miserly. You would deny me everything of beauty and loveliness, while other women of my age walk the gardens of the city clothed in rich raiment."

A colourful satin caftan, produced for the court of Ottoman sultan Ibrahim I (reigned 1640–1648).

And she began to weep. And as her tears fell upon her breast she cried out again, "You always say, 'Nay, nay' to me when I desire a garment or a jewel."

Then the husband was moved, and he stood up and took out of his purse a handful of gold and placed it before her, saying in a kindly voice, "Go down to the market place, my dear, and buy all that you will."

From that day onward the deaf young wife, whenever she desired anything, would appear before her husband with a pearly tear in her eye, and he in silence would take out a handful of gold and place it in her lap.

Now, it chanced that the young woman fell in love with a youth whose habit it was to make long journeys. And whenever he was away she would sit in her casement and weep.

When her husband found her thus weeping, he would say in his heart, "There must be some new caravan, and some silken garments and rare jewels in the Street."

And he would take a handful of gold and place it before her.

The River

In the valley of Kadisha where the mighty river flows, two little streams met and spoke to one another.

One stream said, "How came you, my friend, and how was your path?"

And the other answered, "My path was most encumbered. The wheel of the mill was broken, and the master farmer who used to conduct me from my channel to his plants, is dead. I struggled down oozing with the filth of those who do naught but sit and bake their laziness in the sun. But how was your path, my brother?"

And the other stream answered and said, "Mine was a different path. I came down the hills among fragrant flowers and shy willows; men and women drank of me with silvery cups, and little children paddled their rosy feet at my edges, and there was laughter all about me, and there were sweet songs. What a pity that your path was not so happy."

At that moment the river spoke with a loud voice and said, "Come in, come in, we are going to the sea. Come in, come in, speak no more. Be with me now. We are going to the sea. Come in, come in, for in me you shall forget you wanderings, sad or gay. Come in, come in. And you and I will forget all our ways when we reach the heart of our mother the sea."

Chronology

1883 – On 6 January 1883 Gibran Khalil Gibran, who became known as Kahlil Gibran, is born in Bisharri, Lebanon.

1895 – Gibran emigrates with his family to the United States.

1904 – On 30 April 1904 he exhibits his illustrations in Boston.

1905 – *al-Musiqah* (*Music*) becomes his first published work.

1908 – Gibran studies in Paris.

1911 – Gibran moves to Greenwich Village, New York.

1912 – *al-Ajnihah al Mutakassirah* (*The Broken Wings*) is published to wide acclaim in the Arab world.

1914 – His first major exhibition opens at the Montross Gallery, New York.

1918 – *The Madman* becomes his first published work in English.

1920 – al-Rabita al-Qalamiyyah-Arrabitah (The Pen Bond) is formed by Gibran and seven other Arab writers living in New York, inspiring a renaissance in Arabic literature; *The Forerunnner* is published in New York.

1923 – *The Prophet* is published in New York.

1928 – *Jesus, the Son of Man* is published in New York.

1930 – *The Earth Gods* and *The Wanderer* are published in New York.

1931 – Gibran dies on 10 April 1931 at St Vincent's Hospital, New York, aged forty-eight.

Further Reading

Bushrui, Suheil and Munro J.M. (eds.) *Kahlil Gibran: Essays and Introductions*. Rihani House: Beirut, 1970.

Bushrui, Suheil and Mutlak A. (eds.) *In Memory of Kahlil Gibran: The First Colloquium on Gibran Studies*. Librairie du Liban: Oxford, 1981.

Bushrui, Suheil. *Kahlil Gibran of Lebanon: A Re-evaluation of the Life and Work of the Author of The Prophet*. C. Smythe: Gerrard's Cross, 1987.

Bushrui, Suheil and al-Kuzbari, Salma Haffar. (trans. and eds.) *Gibran Love Letters*. Oneworld: Oxford, 1995.

Bushrui, Suheil and Jenkins, Joe. *Kahlil Gibran, Man and Poet: A New Biography*. Oneworld: Oxford, 1998.

Daoudi, M.S. *The Meaning of Kahlil Gibran*. Citadel Press: Secaucus, 1982.

Ghougassian, J.P. *Kahlil Gibran: Wings of Thought*. Philosophical Library: New York, 1973.

Gibran, J. and K. *Kahlil Gibran: His Life and World*. New York Graphic Society: Boston, 1974.

Hawi, K.S. *Khalil Gibran: His Background, Character and Works*. American University of Beirut: Beirut, 1972.

Hilu, V. (ed.) *Beloved Prophet: The Love Letters of Kahlil Gibran and Mary Haskell and her Private Journal*. Alfred A. Knopf: New York, 1972.

Huwayik, Yusef. *Gibran in Paris*. Popular Library: New York, 1976.

Jayyusi, Salma Khadra. *Trends and Movements in Modern Arabic Poetry*. E.J. Brill: Leiden, 1977.

Kheirallah, G. "The Life of Gibran Khalil Gibran" in *The Procession*. Philosophical Library: New York, 1958.

Naimy, Mikhail. *Kahlil Gibran: A Biography*. Philosophical Library: New York, 1985.

Otto, A.S. *The Parables of Kahlil Gibran*. Citadel Press, New York, 1963

Sherfan, Andrew Deeb. *Kahlil Gibran: The Nature of Love.* Philosophical Library: New York, 1971.

Wolf, M.L. Preface to *Secrets of The Heart* by Kahlil Gibran. Signet: New York, 1965.

Gibran, Kahlil, works in Arabic:

al-Ajnihah al-Mutakassirah (*The Broken Wings*). Miriat al-Gharb: New York, 1912.

al-Arwah al-Mutamarridah (*Spirits Rebellious*). al-Mohajer: New York, 1906.

al-'Awasif (*The Tempests*). al-Hilal: Cairo, 1920.

al-Bayati wa'l-Tarayif (*Beautiful and Rare Sayings*). Maktabti al-'Arb: Cairo, 1923.

al-Mawakib (*The Procession*). Miriat al-Gharb: New York, 1919.

'Ara'is al-Muruj (*Nymphs of the Valley*). al-Mohajer: New York, 1908.

Dam'ah wa Ibtisamah (*A Tear and a Smile*). Miriat al-Gharb: New York, 1914.

Gibran, Kahlil, works in English:

Jesus, the Son of Man: His Words and Deeds as Told and Recorded by Those Who Knew Him. Alfred A. Knopf: New York, 1928. William Heinemann: London, 1928.

The Earth Gods. Alfred A. Knopf: New York, 1930.

The Forerunner: His Parables and Poems. Alfred A. Knopf: New York, 1920. William Heinemann: London, 1921.

The Garden of The Prophet. Alfred A. Knopf: New York, 1931. William Heinemann: London, 1935.

The Madman. Alfred A. Knopf: New York, 1918. William Heinemann: London, 1918.

The Prophet. Alfred A. Knopf: New York, 1923. William Heinemann: London, 1926.

Sand and Foam. Alfred A. Knopf: New York, 1926. William Heinemann: London, 1927.

The Wanderer: His Parables and his Sayings. Alfred A. Knopf: New York, 1930. William Heinemann: London, 1933.

Index

Bahá, Abdu'l 17
beauty 125–127, 178
being 177–178
Bernhardt, Sarah 17
Bisharri, Lebanon 7, 8, 20
Boston, United States of America 9–10
buying and selling 69–70

Chesterton, G.K. 17
children 43–44
clothes 67, 175–176
crime and punishment 73–77

death 133–134, 187
Debussy, Claude 17
desire 37, 260–263
disciples 159, 179, 183, 187
dreams 161, 165–166

Earth Gods, The 19
eating and drinking 51–52

Forerunner, The 13
forerunners 220–223
freedom 83–84, 153, 232
friendship 101–102, 246–251

Galsworthy, John 17
Garden of the Prophet, The 19, 20
Gibran, Kahlil
    art 9–10
    birth 7
    death 20

emigration, to the United States of America 9
    later life 17–21
    works 11–21
Gibran, Kahlil (father) 8, 9
giving 47–49, 142, 185–186
    and receiving 164
    knowledge 180–183
God 172–175, 192–194
    knowledge of 130
god-self 73
good and evil 113–115

Haskell, Mary 10, 11, 13, 14, 16
hell 175
hermits, wisdom of 226–229
houses 63–65

Iram, The City of Lofty Pillars 16

Jesus, the Son of Man 18
joy and sorrow 59–60, 214
Jung, Carl Gustav 17

knowledge 140

laws 79–80
Lebanon 7–9, 11, 17, 20
life 156–158
    and death 171–172, 264
loneliness 170–171
love 15, 35–37, 109, 224
    for humankind 234–239
    in friendship 101, 246–251

in marriage 39
in work 55–57
pain of 35

Madman, The 12, 16
man, nature of 196–199,
    206–209, 216–219
Maronite Christians 8, 11
marriage 39–40
mist 153, 188–189

nakedness 175–176
New York 10–11
New York Times, The 15–16
Nietzsche, Friedrich 10
night and the soul 202–205
Nymphs of the Valley 11

Orozco, José Clemente 17

pain 91–92
parasitism 168–169
Paris 10
passion and reason 87–89
pleasure 121–123
poetry 246
possessions 47
prayer 117–119
Prophet, The 14–17

Rahmeh, Kamileh (mother) 8, 9
reason and passion 87–89
religion 129–130
Russell, George (AE) 16

Sand and Foam 18
self-knowledge 95–96
solitude 170–171, 232
sorrow 59–60, 214

soul 95–96, 179
    nature of 240–245
Spirits Rebellious 11
Sufism 12, 16

talking 105–106, 176–177
teaching 99
Tempests, The 11
time 109–110, 167

ugliness 166–167
United States of America
    criticism of life and politics
        159–161
    Gibran's life 9–20

Wanderer, The 19–20
wanderers 137
wisdom 140, 210
    aphorisms 252–257
words 176–177
work 55–57
World War One 11, 12

Yeats, W.B. 17

Picture Credits

The publisher would like to thank the following people, museums and photographic libraries for permission to reproduce their material. Every care has been taken to trace copyright holders. However, if we have omitted anyone we apologize and will, if informed, make corrections to any future edition.

AA = Art Archive, London
AKG = AKG-images, London
BAL = Bridgeman Art Library, London
BL = The British Library, London
BM = © Trustees of the British Museum, London
IOA = Institute of Oriental Art, Chicago
MC = Musée Condé, Chantilly
MIK = Museum für Islamische Kunst, Staatliche Museen zu Berlin
ML = Musée du Louvre, Paris
MS = Musée National de Céramique, Sèvres
RMN = Réunion des Musées Nationaux, Paris
TSM = Topkapi Saray Müzesi, Istanbul
V&A = Victoria and Albert Museum/V&A Images, London
WFA = Werner Forman Archive, London

Page 2 V&A; 6 V&A; 26 ML/RMN – ©Jean-Gilles Berizzi; 31 Turkish and Islamic Art Museum, Istanbul/AA/A Dagli Orti; 34 Getty/Iconica/Frank Whitney; 38 Photolibrary.com/Nordicphotos/Bjorn Wiklander; 41 ML/RMN – ©Hervé Lewandowski; 42 Archaeological Museum, Teheran/WFA; 45 ML/RMN – ©Michel Urtado; 46 Mosaic Museum, Istanbul/WFA; 50 BM; 53 Oriental Museum, Durham University/BAL; 54 Getty/Iconica/Fernand Ivaldi; 58 V&A; 61 MIK/WFA; 62 Corbis/Christophe Boisvieux; 64 BM; 66 MS/AA/Dagli Orti; 68 Bibliotheque Nationale, Paris/AKG; 71 Corbis/Farrell Grehan; 72 ML/RMN – ©Hervé Lewandowski; 76 AKG/Stefan Drechsel; 78 ML/RMN – ©Hervé Lewandowski; 81 Corbis/Arthur Thévenart; 82 MC/AA/Dagli Orti; 85 Getty/Photographer's Choice/Paul Souders; 86 Corbis/Diane Cook & Len Jenshel; 88 MIK/BAL; 90 MIK/WFA; 93 ML/RMN – ©Franck Raux; 94 Corbis/André Burian; 97 Rockefeller Museum (IDAM), Jerusalem/AKG/Erich Lessing; 98 BL/AA; 100 Getty/Image Bank/Loungepark; 103 Musée National de la Renaissance, Ecouen/RMN

Acknowledgments

The publishers would like to thank Professor Suheil Bushrui for his advice and assistance during the early development of this project. The text is reproduced from editions originally published in the United Kingdom from 1918 to 1935. New text material is contained in the Introduction and caption illustrations (where appropriate).